THE FORSAKEN IDEA

THE
FORSAKEN IDEA

A Study of
VISCOUNT MILNER

by

EDWARD CRANKSHAW

GREENWOOD PRESS, PUBLISHERS
WESTPORT, CONNECTICUT

Library of Congress Cataloging in Publication Data

Crankshaw, Edward.
    The forsaken idea.

    Reprint of the 1952 ed. published by Longmans, Green,
London.
    1. Milner, Alfred Milner, 1st Viscount, 1854-1925.
2. Africa, South--History. I. Title.
[DT776.M6C7 1974]   325.342'0968'7   73-17918
ISBN 0-8371-7278-0

First published in 1952 by Longmans, Green and Co., London

Reprinted with the permission of Edward Crankshaw

Reprinted in 1974 by Greenwood Press,
a division of Williamhouse-Regency Inc.

Library of Congress Catalogue Card Number 73-17918

ISBN 0-8371-7278-0

Printed in the United States of America

For Viscountess Milner
in gratitude and
devotion

AUTHOR'S NOTE

References to the sources of all quotations will be found in the text where they occur. But I wish particularly to thank Lady Milner for permission to quote freely from various published and unpublished sources, and for her generous help.

I must acknowledge a special debt to the late Cecil Headlam for his editorial work in *Milner Papers* (Messrs. Cassell & Co., Ltd.).

My thanks are also due to the publishers of two of Lord Milner's books for permission to quote from them: *Nation and Empire* (Messrs. Constable & Co., Ltd.), and *Questions of the Hour* (Messrs. Hodder & Stoughton Ltd.).

Finally I should like to record the titles of certain other books referred to in the text: *England in Egypt* by Lord Milner (Messrs. Edward Arnold & Co.); *Lord Milner and South Africa* by E. A. Walker (Oxford University Press); and *On England and other Addresses* by Lord Baldwin (Philip Allan).

E.C.

CONTENTS

FOREWORD

THIS BOOK IS not a biography of Lord Milner, who wished that no biography of himself should be written. It is a sketch of his ideas, as reflected in his own writings and speeches and in his actions, especially in South Africa, and with particular regard to their relevance to our own problems. Few great men have had to suffer such universal misunderstanding of their own motives and ideas. We too have suffered from our own failure to understand. I have tried to indicate how much by quoting from nothing (apart from a few private letters and extracts from Lord Milner's diary) which has not been available in published form for many years. Thus, the line of thought which I have tried to isolate is not a new discovery and does not in the least depend for its effect on the mass of unpublished papers covering the later years. My own introduction to Lord Milner's mind was effected through his published papers; and the impact of these was marked by a sense of shock that ideas so lucidly expressed and so immediately relevant to our own time should have been for so long ignored. If this inadequate and belated tribute will send readers to Lord Milner's own writings while there is still a little time to profit by them, it will have served its only purpose.

Finally, it will almost certainly be pointed out that this book is biased. The opposition side of the case has held the field and conditioned the minds of successive generations for half a century. We may be said to know it.

EDWARD CRANKSHAW

August 1951

PART ONE
THE MAN

Chapter One

UNREPRESENTATIVE MEN

IN THE SWEPT and shadowless arena of the historians there occur here and there, scattered through the time-dimension, figures whose faces are not clear. They occur in every generation. They are of all kinds, beneficent and sinister. They will not fit into the historian's pattern because in life they did not fit perfectly into their own time. Only the creative artist can safely indulge this awkwardness, knowing that history will catch up with his achievement and arrange the setting to cause the jewel, obscured in life, to blaze with reflected light. But others besides artists have a time-defying quality, which is apparent neither in their work, because this lacks the comparative permanence of a work of art, nor in their biographies, because they are not representative figures of their age. It lives on, nevertheless, frequently unsuspected, more often than not unacknowledged, in the influence exercised in their lifetimes over the men they worked with, and, through them, passed on. Lord Milner was one of these.

His failure to fit into his own time was not complete. In many ways, indeed, he was very much of his own time, when his most influential contemporaries were not. If anything, he failed in communication. Wherever he looked he saw individual problems of great complexity, often unsuspected by others; he found reasonable solutions to many of these problems, all within the framework of one general solution. But he lacked the power to communicate the reality and urgency of those problems to others, who saw only his solutions—solutions to problems which they themselves had not at all envisaged, but which then existed in embryo and have now grown to overwhelm us. He himself, believing imperiously in the power of reason, though not in the

3

reasonableness of men, almost certainly ignored the immense part played in his own attitude to affairs by intuition. Thus many of his actions sprang from a profound instinct, unseen by the world, which only saw the actions, and probably only half realised by himself. Thus his advocacy of force in dealing with the Boers had its roots not so much in the immediate reasons given by him, but in his profound concern with the ultimate survival of Great Britain. Again, he fitted into no party pattern, not because he was neither hot nor cold, nor because he habitually saw more than one side to every question (which in fact he did), nor because he lacked deep convictions one way or the other, nor even because he could not agree with all the tenets of a single party, but rather because the main preoccupations of all the parties at that moment in English history when the English party system was supposed to have reached its zenith, seemed to him irrelevant and vain. Not that he held aloof from party. On the contrary: in the end he worked for the Conservatives. Not because he was one with them in all their ideas: he fought their ideas for all he was worth on what to him were all-important questions of domestic and social policy. But he found, as some are finding today, that the Conservatives were the only people it was possible to work with. They were possible to work with because they remained human beings. They regarded politics as a means, not as an end; they were empirical and not doctrinaire; there were always some among them who could, in any crisis, take a deep breath and look round with an open mind for new ideas. At their worst they stood for mental atrophy, selfishness and moral sloth; but at their best, and in essence, they reflected with accuracy the English temperament, or character, for better or for worse, and in clear opposition to what one may call the Continental strain of intellectual determinism which runs through both Liberalism and Socialism of all kinds.

When Milner spoke, as he did, of the comparative ease with which he could work with Conservatives, he was speaking as an Englishman first, as a politician afterwards. His interests had, in fact, purged themselves into a single over-ruling passion: a passion for the survival of this country with its sister nations and dependent Empire. He was not alone in his patriotism: to a greater or less degree it was shared by most Conservatives and many Liberals. But before and after the First World War he was almost entirely alone in the urgency of his patriotism. That is to say, for the great majority of his contemporaries, patriotism was not a vital issue: it was something to be taken for granted. It was not, as it was for the French, a burning question, with the survival of the country in the balance. There could, in the popular mind, be no question of failure to survive. England was England: that was the fixed point round which the world revolved. Granted this pre-Copernican attitude, patriotism was not a thing to make a fuss about. It was even a thing to despise. For no matter how fast and loose you played, there would always be an England.

This blessed assurance has now departed from us. The question of the survival of England—as an independent power certainly, as a nation probably—has, in a rush, become for us all the question of the hour. *Questions of the Hour* was the title of a small book of essays which Milner published in 1923 shortly before his death. Most of the views put forward in it were then of a highly pro- vocative kind. They were, indeed, so provocative that they were almost at once forgotten. Today, however, many of these views have already been absorbed into the fabric of our thought; and others very soon will be. So that what Milner had to say, twenty- eight years ago, about what seemed to him the most immediate problems, surpasses in relevance to our own troubles the greater part of what is being written today. So one is driven to conclude that many of our own problems are no more than the changing superficial aspects of more lasting problems which have not changed much in the last twenty-five years, in spite of the atom- bomb and Moscow Communism.

We are talking of political problems, not of the eternal verities. And reading Milner today brings home very sharply the per- manence of political problems. This is familiar to all who read history; but, as a rule, distance puts our study outside the circle of immediate actuality. Milner, who died only twenty-five years ago, brings history into our own time and turns the present into history. He himself made no such claim. He would have called himself a man of affairs who found time to think. It would be better to call him an original thinker who was also a brilliant man of affairs. He was acutely conscious of that chaos which perplexed his own contemporaries, as our own particular chaos bears down upon us and perplexes us. He saw himself always as a man groping through a dark wood.

Looking back at that modest volume of reflections on our condition published shortly before his death, it is now easy to see that the supreme question indicated by the title was, precisely, whether and how this country could survive. And this questioning was simply the extension of all that he had striven for during a strenuous career in which he was touched by the extremes of praise and blame without being moved by either.

Almost certainly Milner never put that question in so many words. But it was behind everything he said or did. He was enough of a philosopher to know that empires fall and that the British Empire was not exempt from the breath of common mortality; he was enough of a realist to see that Britain, alone, could never regain her unchallenged and effortless supremacy, that she could, at the most, hope henceforth to sustain a proud position as leader of the Empire, and thus as one world power among equals; he was enough of an economist to realise that England had to be great or nothing, and could never, even if she willed it, cosily subside into a Scandinavian neutrality; he was enough of an Englishman to desire, with passion, the survival of his country and his people; and he was enough of a sceptic to ask whether their survival was desirable. It is thus easy to see where he failed to fit into his own time. Far more importantly, it makes him a man of our own time, a man of freer intellect than any practising politician we now have with us, and above all a contemporary who had, as it were, a pre-view of our present distress and told us how to avoid at least a great part of it.

That is why a consideration of the thought and character of a most exceptional statesman, born before his time, who died twenty-five years ago while still actively engaged with problems which most of us ignored until a year or two ago, is surely not irrelevant. It is not suggested that Milner can be made to solve our problems for us; but it is suggested that he can help us to get into a proper frame of mind for tackling them seriously ourselves.

There is a rare type of mind which applies itself instinctively to life as a whole and sees it all of a piece. One may differ from any or all of the conclusions reached by an intelligence of this kind; but, once encountered, it can never be forgotten, and no problem is clearly seen until it is looked at in the light of that mind. Milner's mind was one of these.

Chapter Two

PATRIOT AND SCEPTIC

HE WAS AN Imperialist. Since nobody has yet shown how this small, over-populated, over-industrialised island is expected to survive without Imperial interests, this is not surprising. He took his Imperialism for granted, the interesting question for him being: what kind of Imperialism? His unfaltering patriotism did not always come easily, since few men have had a keener appreciation of the shortcomings of the British; and all his life he was engaged in working out a running answer to the question why a race capable of such enormities and inanities, such stupidities and such treacheries in its dealings with foreigners, its enemies and its friends (above all its friends), should be considered worth preserving. For behind the proconsular exterior was the free mind of the artist and the shrewd detachment of the dispassionate critic of mankind. He saw very straight and very quickly. His thought in a professional thinker or historian, calm and unharassed in the white circle of the reading-lamp, would have been remarkable for its depth and speed and straightness. In a statesman and administrator, fighting always against odds of some kind and burdened with the clutter of detailed decisions, it is more than remarkable. It was as though a Balfour had exchanged his sense of fun for a sense of responsibility. He could, in a single phrase, fire a spreading sequence of new ideas: 'I look forward to the time when instead of Capital hiring Labour, Labour should hire Capital.' He could see through a sacred institution without realising the depth of his penetration: 'Lancashire is not Free Trade', he wrote in one of his notebooks; 'Lancashire is cotton, and especially cotton export. Once let there be cotton imports into this country . . . and Lancashire would be Protectionist.' He concealed his originality of mind so

8

sedulously from the world, holding very properly that intellectual
fireworks in a statesman are not calculated to win the confidence
of the country or the respect of his colleagues, that, to judge from
his published writings, his thought might seem pedestrian and
his humour weak. Even when close attention to his greyly
expressed ideas makes it quite clear that they are soaring far above
the earth, so neutral is the tone that one would be forgiven for
wondering whether Milner himself quite knew what he was
doing.

But that he was aware of his isolation and detachment and
therefore, by implication, of the originality of his politics, is
shown in little flashes in his private correspondence and far more
in the reminiscences of those who knew him and lived with him.
Thus, of the man who could observe flatly that Lancashire was
not free trade, but only cotton export, it would be tempting to
write that he was an unconscious incarnation of the man who
could not see the Emperor's new clothes: admirable but a little
dull. Until, suddenly, we find in a letter to Lady Edward Cecil,
whom, after a life-long friendship, he was to marry in his closing
years: 'I seem to be the lineal descendant of the child who could
not see the Emperor's fine clothes.' And, as suddenly, the man
comes alive and interesting, complicated and formidably human,
no longer the neutral mouthpiece of inspired common sense, but
something much more subtle and attractive.

His attitude towards politics, always latent, seems to have
crystallised out during his South African years. By temperament
and nature he was the man on the spot, the field-commander as
opposed to the man at a headquarters desk. But by training and
mental equipment he was the supreme headquarters man. This
contradiction must often have led to inner conflict; but in the end
it was the man on the spot whom he trusted and the Whitehall
official, entangled inevitably, whether passively or actively,
reluctantly or enthusiastically, in political intrigue, upon whom
he turned his back. He was the man on the spot in Egypt; and
then, after years at the Board of Inland Revenue, he became the
man on the spot in South Africa. His letters and instructions to his
own subordinates scattered on their lonely stations in South Africa,

even more than his despatches to Whitehall, show time and time again how deeply he felt his responsibility towards his job, as distinct from his employers in Whitehall, and how thoroughly he identified himself in Cape Town with the cares and individual responsibilities of his outposts. At that time Cape Town, like Cairo in the late war, invited development into a remote headquarters, in which anyone might be forgiven for looking back over his shoulder to Whitehall instead of straight ahead at his work and his men in the field. It was this quality which explained the loyalty of Milner's subordinates and the place he held in their mind: so that during one of his absences in England, Goold Adams, the Governor of the Orange Free State, wrote: 'Africa feels empty without Milner.' It was this quality, also, which explained his readiness to fight the Boers. It is easy to practise a slippery policy at long range—an exercise in which British Government offices have always excelled—perhaps because the foreigner, thanks to geography, is always at long range. But on the ground and with your opponent confronting you, there is no room for highfalutin manœuvring under the general head of compromise: either you give way or the other fellow gives way, and the one thing to be cherished, like the sword in its scabbard, is the pledged word, the only weapon you have except, in the last resort, the sword itself. After one of his rare disagreements with Joseph Chamberlain, Milner was to write: '. . . All interferences from home are bad. I resist as long as I can. When resistance is hopeless, I give way on minor points. I am prepared to make small mistakes to please them. No man can expect to have all his own way. But I will not be their agent for big mistakes. If they are set on such they must find another agent. . . .'

But more characteristic even than his attitude towards the Boers was his behaviour over the question of Chinese labour in South Africa. To call any man responsible for the Boer War is out of the question. Sooner or later we should have had to fight or leave South Africa altogether; and the Imperial interests at work to keep us in South Africa were beyond the power of any man to work against, even had it been desirable. The Chinese labour question, on the other hand, displayed Milner in his strength and his weakness. During his great period of reconstruction after the Peace of Vereeniging he had to make a success of the Transvaal or abandon the whole field. But the Rand, upon which the Transvaal economy hung, could not be run without cheap labour of a particular kind. In the Chinese coolie such labour existed and demanded employment. The logic of the situation was to employ it. This Milner did, with the expressed agreement of the moderate Liberal leaders, bringing about such an outcry in the less moderate Liberal Press and Parliamentary Opposition that at the very height of his fame he was broken, or so the world thought: in fact he was very far from broken. But the point to be made is that in that situation we see the whole man: the power to think straight; the character, or the strength of will, to abide by the conclusion reached; and the failure to reckon with muddled thinking in others as a fact of life, no less real than malice.

It should not be assumed, however, that his particular mixture of logic, steadfastness, intellectual integrity and decision invariably landed him in trouble. Far from it. Perhaps the most striking of all his exercises in this manner, and certainly one of the most fruitful of good, was when as a member of the War Cabinet in 1918 he signed Foch into the supreme command, as it were between lunch and tea. In the eye-witness accounts of this episode what is chiefly remarkable is the total absence of argumentation, of fuss, of face-saving reservations. Milner knew very well that he could carry Lloyd George with him—as certainly as he could know anything. But in those terrible hours after the collapse of the Fifth Army, alone, a British politician among soldiers, he behaved as few subordinates have ever behaved in matters of great weight, never for one moment raising a doubt in the minds of the soldiers, never hesitating to do the logical thing as quickly as he could think it, and fully prepared to take on himself responsibility for failure. There was no failure. Had there been, the responsibility would have been his and his alone. But the credit for success could not be his.

Chapter Three

FIRST PROMISE

IN ORDER TO appreciate the weight of Milner's thought about the survival of Britain and the British Empire, to say nothing about his remarkable achievement, it is necessary to know something of his origins and also of his attitude towards life in general. For Milner was not born into a family of philistines; and his thoughts on questions other than the preservation of the British Empire were not the thoughts of the traditional ruling class. The point here to be made is that his Imperialism was the outcome not of training but of original thinking; and it was the same with all his beliefs. What is above all interesting is that in his mind the sort of attitude loosely and disastrously dismissed as jingoism for the last half-century may be seen, in essentials, to have been more of a piece with a free and experimental approach to the problems of government than with the conventional limitations of the normal public-school mentality. It is this last which is usually equated, quite without grounds, with the more positive forms of patriotism. And, indeed, here is the fallacy which lies behind much of our present distress, care of country and of Empire having been left by those who can read Shakespeare (and yet miss so much of what he stood for) to those who cannot read Shakespeare at all: in a word, to precisely that class of mentality least qualified to appreciate the true nature and demands of those most subtle and fluid conceptions.

Milner came to them with a fresh mind of great tenacity and power. He was born of British parents in Germany, at Bonn, on March 23rd, 1854, and his first thirty years were filled with scarcely interrupted struggle, sustained by a native seriousness of purpose which was itself strengthened by the terms of his battle with life. Such a struggle and such seriousness, however, can never be borne by any but the third-rate without constant renewal from within. And such self-renewal is the gift only of those who, behind no matter what sort of an appearance they may find it convenient to present to the world, preserve the gaiety and spontaneity of absolute youth. This may perhaps be defined as an unquestioning and instinctive acceptance of the provisional and makeshift character of all human knowledge and activity. Thus, what matters in the eyes of such men is not the game itself but the spirit in which it is conducted and obedience to the rules. The game may be absurd: we have no means of knowing. But it has to be played, and everything depends on the way it is played. In many societies, and particularly in our own, children are said to be grown up when they have reached the stage of forgetting that the game they happen to be engaged in is only one of many.

Milner never committed this vulgarity. Like all other great men (as distinct from the great virtuosi, such as Napoleon or Frederick), whether successful in a worldly sense or not, he retained the detachment and mental freedom of his childhood. And this, even in his days of most bitter responsibility, as during the Boer War and in the closing stages of the 1914 war, would manifest itself when off duty in a total lack of self-importance and pomposity, a profound and unquestioning modesty, an unquenchable sense of fun, and a delight in the company of simple souls. His public reputation for extreme thoroughness, unbending rigidity of outlook, a humourless and bleak approach to life, was due partly to the accident of a rather grand physical appearance and partly to the exact reverse of what was commonly suspected: namely, an absence of any thought for his own importance, which went with an acute sense of the importance of his job. His German birth, the facts of which were distorted, then exaggerated, helped to confirm and strengthen this impression.

In fact, his father was an English physician, his mother the widow of an Irishman and the daughter of Major-General Ready, sometime governor of Prince Edward Island and of the Isle of Man. Only his paternal grandmother was a German; but a good deal of his education was received in Germany, where he lived until he was four and then, again, from twelve to fifteen, with frequent visits thereafter. He was close enough to the Teutonic mind to delight in its positive contribution to civilisation, but not to be entangled in its grosser fallacies.

From his father he inherited no streak of Teutonic thoroughness. Indeed, the somewhat bleak, pursuing air which his enemies were to mark in him much later might better be seen as the outcome of reaction against his father's carelessness. For Dr. Milner was brilliance itself, who could never make medicine a first claim on his life, preferring open-air pursuits of every kind, and, after these, Shakespeare, Goethe, and the classics. His son inherited his love of physical exercises and, in the manner of our fathers, tubbed and walked and swam at all times and with energy: with a different social background he would have joined a cycling club. There is also a foretaste of the son in Dr. Milner's contempt of all humbug, a contempt for which he gladly paid the price by refusing to treat his patients for imaginary illnesses, thus reducing his Chelsea practice to next to nothing at all. It was this process which sent him back to Germany as Reader in English Literature at Tübingen when Alfred was twelve years old. Alfred, having more or less automatically become head of his London day-school in Eaton Square, should have gone on to Rugby; but in spite of his mental robustness and physical energy, his health was delicate, and, because of this, Rugby was abandoned and for the next four years, until soon after his mother's death, he went as a day-boy to the Tübingen Gymnasium.

From the age of sixteen, after the death of his mother, whom he adored and whose memory was to dominate his life, he had to depend upon himself alone. When one looks at the record of the influential friends to whom he was to owe so much during the years that followed, the first thought is that nobody could have been given a better start in life than this youngster of extreme promise surrounded and upheld by devoted seniors. But although he owed much to his friends, to Professor Mayor at King's College, to Jowett at Balliol, to Arnold Toynbee and Lord Goschen, he owed these friends to no one but himself. That is to say, he inherited no influence: he acquired it by being what he was and attracting the devotion of those who were able to help him—just as, in later life, in Egypt and South Africa, he attracted the devotion of so many brilliant younger men and helped to make them as he himself had been made. In considering the record of Milner's actions and in contemplating the image of those grave and angular features, emphasised by the drooping moustache, it is necessary to remember always that no man has ever shown a greater power of attracting friends from every walk of life, and holding them. To begin with it was done, as it were, on a shoe-string.

For Milner, at sixteen, had nothing, and nobody but a handful of family friends, whom he cherished but who could do little for him. His mother, dying, did what she could, determined to get that brilliant promise away from Germany. But after some months at King's College under the care of relatives, further bereavement left him alone but for a cousin of thirty-one, and at the same time showed him that the greater part of his small inheritance from his mother had been lost. He had to choose between going back to Tübingen and his father or staying on at King's College sharing a struggling *ménage* with his cousin. He chose the latter, although bitterly lonely and detesting the cooped-up life in London. A little later, looking round for the best scholarship to Oxford, he was put on to the Balliol which, at eighteen, he sat for and won, reducing his expenditure on essentials in order to pay for his coaching. This first great victory seems to have had an effect of release on the spirit of one who had worked too hard, and alone, for too long. He was an undergraduate at once, and although he had to watch every penny, and was indeed at first disconcerted by the amplitude of his Balliol rooms, which somehow had to be furnished, and although work had to come first and did come first, his letters to a cousin at that time do not in the least reflect the spirit of the lugubrious 'swot'. Indeed, he could already take a perfectly detached and ironic view of himself, and the difference between his own view of himself in moments of depression and his repeated performance was remarkable. 'I thought myself a beaten "Scholarship-hunter,"' he wrote of his mood after sitting for the Balliol scholarship, 'with no ultimate hope but mediocrity.' And this recurrent self-depreciation was never to leave him entirely. While at Balliol, at that time at the peak of its reputation, with Asquith, Charles Gore, Toynbee, and others to compete with, he won the Hertford, Craven, Eldon and Derby scholarships; but the Ireland he missed through despair:

> . . . If you know what it is to be very disappointed without being at all disheartened you know my present state of mind [he wrote to his cousin, Miss Malcolm]. The fact is I have lost the 'Ireland' and lost it by accident. I must tell you the whole story. The first three days I got on well, worked hard, saw my way clearly and was satisfied. But by this time I had got all the work that was in me out of myself. The next day I felt my head muddled and the morning of the fifth day—we had Greek verses in which I rather hoped to score —I could do simply nothing. I was excited and forgetful. After an hour and a half I got up, tore up my papers and walked off, walked out into the country and hoped to hear no more about the 'Ireland'. That night, when I came in, Jowett sent for me and struck me all of a heap by telling me that I had been a long way ahead, as long as I was in, and if I could but have shown up some papers, *any* papers that last day, the thing would have been mine. . . . Jowett was so awfully kind about it, that I nearly cried at him. He told me that I had done brilliantly and that I was to try and forget everything about it except those first days of success. 'It can make no difference to you in life,' he said as I left him. 'You have a splendid career before you and this disappointment is no more than a passing disappointment, after all.'

The losing of the Ireland certainly made no difference to him in life. It was immediately followed by a first in Greats, a Fellowship at New College, and the Craven scholarship. But the strain in him that caused him to lose the Ireland did, almost certainly, make a difference to him in life. It had a good deal to do with his long retirement from affairs between his return from South Africa in 1905 and his call to the Cabinet in 1916. At the time he wrote of that retirement as a direct consequence of his distaste for politicians. But there was more to it than this. Had Milner been utterly convinced of his true value to the country, he would have carried on. His power of standing up to adverse criticism when he considered himself in the right was unlimited, though there is no doubt that he suffered under it more than he ever showed. Throughout the venomous attacks of the pro-Boers in South Africa before the war and of the British Liberal Press later on, he exhibited a cool and unruffled bearing which gave his enemies nothing to get hold of and thus exacerbated their generalised fury. 'Sir, you must have the hide of an alligator!' exclaimed an American enthusiast during this period; and this man of extreme sensitiveness was delighted with the compliment. 'Pray to God to be delivered from the fear of the opinions of those whose deeds have proved them worthless', he once wrote in his first year at Oxford. And, in the words of Mr. Cecil Headlam, '... once he had made up his mind as to what was right, the criticism of those whose mentality or motives he had reason to distrust weighed with him not at all'. Thus it seems that the motive which drove him to tear up his papers for the Ireland and, many years later, to retire from public life was not in any way due to a fear of the world but to doubts about his own ability to deflect it.

In order to carry on he had to be absolutely convinced of his own utility: then he could withstand the most brutal trials. But doubt was never far away, and when it approached too close it would overcome his natural confidence; and then nothing in the world could make him continue the struggle. He had to be sure.

'Would you be surprised to hear that I have got the Hertford?' he wrote from Oxford. 'I feel that I have a very great deal to thank God for and that once more there is reposed in me a great trust. These things stagger one at first. One does not realise them. One can only hope that with the gradual realisation of success may come also a profounder feeling of duty. . . . I am not very religious, but I do feel now and hope I may remember, that these gifts are only valuable, if one uses them for some unselfish end.'

Seven years later, and in the same spirit, he decided to give up the Bar as a career and go where duty called. Then he wrote in his private diary for December 16th, 1881: 'Well, my mind is made up. Resolution fixed. Bar thrown overboard. Off I go upon the wide ocean. If I live to 50 years it will be interesting to look back and see whither my venture has carried me. At any rate, as long as I keep my health—and if I lose it there is my fellowship to live on—I have nothing to fear in a life, the first condition of which is celibacy. One cannot have everything. I am a poor man and must choose between public usefulness and private happiness. I choose the former, or rather I choose to strive for it.'

Without in the least trespassing on the grounds of the metaphysicians and asking, for example, whether choice plays any part in such a decision, we can establish one thing: namely, that at twenty-seven Alfred Milner deliberately abandoned the chance of a brilliant professional career to enter, somehow, the public service. He did not then know how. Twenty-five years later he was to retire from public life, turning his back once more on many glittering prizes. He could not, in a word, force his feet to march away from his heart. This conjunction of ambition and absolute sincerity is rare and interesting.

For that he was ambitious is clear from his earliest days. He had to excel. He had to reach the top of the class, the school, the university; and although this imperative was strengthened by poverty, it existed also in its own right. In those early days when Jowett promised him a great career, Ireland or no Ireland, it is likely enough (though we do not know for certain) that he was thinking in terms of, precisely, a career: a career, that is to say, in any honourable profession attainable by one of his qualities and means, which offered promise of self-vindication. For this, more than fame or riches, was almost certainly the spur. The Bar, with journalism as a side line in the early days, was the obvious path. He had no tradition of politics behind him. He was not, even in his Oxford days, a party man. He wanted to shine among his peers, even though none but his peers could register the wavelength of that light. If he looked ahead so far, he may sometimes have seen the Woolsack as his penultimate earthly resting-place. He could as certainly have attained it.

But his ambition was greater than that. He wished to shine, especially in youth; he was consumed with that desire for conquest and, as we have said, self-vindication, which drives other men to die on Everest. But he also wished, and above all, to serve. He was 'not very religious' in his own naïve phrase. But he was always a great deal more conscious than a Lord Chancellor can afford to be of the last earthly resting-place of all and its casual mockery of earthly greatness. He had his own measure of human performance and achievement; and although he never formulated this in so many words, it established itself early in his mind and never left him. It was not the vice-regal measure. Only a fortnight before he took his decision to abandon the Bar he was writing also in his diary:

> It is rather a pity that I can't keep this diary more regularly, as if I could it might throw some light on the great mystery of life—how time ebbs away with nothing to show for it, while all the time one is, it seems to oneself, consummately busy. Here have I been busy for five weeks—and I have done some 38 guineas worth of scribbling in the *Pall Mall*, a little work for A. Cohen exceedingly thin in character. . . . All these things taken together leave me precisely where I was, as far as making any useful or honourable career for myself in the world is concerned. There is still the great problem Bar or no Bar? All that is best in me cries out for the second and yet I have no courage to take the plunge.

Just fourteen days later he found the courage, relying on journalism for a livelihood and hoping that sooner or later some political opening would turn up.

Chapter Four

BACKGROUND OF A STATESMAN

AMBITION IN ITS crude sense was soon to leave him entirely. As he matured, he grew younger; and the years of his apprenticeship to affairs were swept by a high wind of zest and pleasure in doing. The abandonment of the Bar meant that he gave himself increasingly to journalism; and journalism for him meant the *Pall Mall Gazette*, first under Morley, with Stead as assistant editor, then, when Morley went (unable to bear any longer his unnatural partnership with the man who was revolutionising journalism), as assistant editor. For three years Milner worked hand in glove with Stead, ballasting that highly erratic genius. Those years he enjoyed, as he was always to enjoy all things active and new. There was nothing of the 'scholarship hunter' or the grey administrator, still less of the bleak reactionary of later legend, in the enthusiasm with which he flung himself into remodelling the paper when Morley had gone. Furthermore, he stood by his new chief through the episode which turned the world against him—the notorious anti-prostitution campaign, in which the melodramatic streak in the creator of the new journalism defeated his passionately serious and largely exalted purpose, landing him in prison.

But soon after that *débâcle*, Milner was out of journalism for good. Politics were already pulling him towards the vortex of national affairs. In the 1885 General Election, at thirty-one, he fought Harrow for the Liberals and lost. But more important by far than this (which nevertheless gave him his first indication that he was born to be a public figure, if not by any means a demagogue), he began to do part-time secretarial work for G. J. Goschen, who was almost at once to enter the wilderness ot Liberal Unionism after his break with Gladstone over Home

Rule, and in a year or two to become Chancellor of the Exchequer under Salisbury.

Sooner or later Milner would have found himself in some sort of political employment. He would have come to it most naturally through social reform. His association with Goschen, who very quickly recognised his qualities for what they were, meant that he came to it by the faster, surer and less publicised road of financial administration. He had no political affiliations. This man whom a later generation of Liberals was to anathematise as the arch-obstructionist of all 'progressive' ideas, cold, harsh, reactionary, himself first stood for Parliament as a Liberal and had already closely explored the nature of Socialism, to the ordinary politician of those days no more than a bogey. Indeed, as we shall see, he was a good deal closer to the ideals of Socialism until the end of his days than are most of our contemporary trade-unionists.

His practical interest in social reform he owed to his own heart and mind; the canalisation of his thoughts and feelings he owed to Arnold Toynbee, perhaps the greatest formative influence in his life. He had met Toynbee at Balliol and become his intimate, throwing himself into plans for the betterment of the working-man and more general recognition of the dignity of manual labour. Thus it was through Toynbee that Milner, the shining scholar, found himself in the company of Oscar Wilde and Andrew Lang toiling away under Ruskin's direction at the construction of the Hinksey Road. . . . Afterwards he worked with Toynbee in Bermondsey, among other things delivering four elaborate lectures on Socialism, from which we shall later quote. Indeed, he was so much a Toynbee man that he almost felt that Toynbee's death would be the end of life to him. But it was not. Toynbee lived on in Milner, as in so many others.

> His life had unity [he wrote to Mrs. Toynbee some years later from Egypt] and so, despite its lamentable shortness, it produced deep and lasting effects. For one must remember that for every trace of his influence that ever comes to the surface, there were a thousand seeds sown, of which we may not recognise the fruit. All those who knew him well will be infinitely the stronger in the long struggle to hold fast to unselfish objects and ideal aims, which the

daily difficulties of life are always wearing away. . . . I speak of my own experience. I am a man of the world and of affairs, not pretending or seeking to be otherwise, but holding on, not with a relaxing grasp, to my own great link with the higher life to which he belonged and belongs altogether. . . .

It is worth recording at this stage that at the time of Milner's liveliest interest in Socialism the Labour movement had petered out after the fearful trade depressions of the 'seventies and the consequent preoccupation of the unions with emergency rescue work. But in 1881 H. M. Hyndman founded the Social Democratic Federation; in 1883 the Fabian Society first saw light; and in 1892 Keir Hardie, John Burns and Havelock Wilson were returned to Parliament. The new Labour movement was then in full swing. For a young man of brilliant parts and a career to make for himself to be thinking in terms of practical Socialism in the 'eighties, even if only to reject it with some regret, was already proof of extreme independence of mind. At the same time, the embryo Labour movement, with its narrow class interest, was the last thing to attract the allegiance of a man who was already beginning to think in terms not only of Britain but also of Britain's influence for good in the world at large.

If it seems that too much stress has been laid on this particular aspect of Milner's mind, the point has not been made clear. For the point is that Milner's rejection of a professional career, his veneration of Toynbee, and his early grasp of Socialism—together with his rejection of it as the best way towards social reform—was not by any means a particular aspect. It was the whole man. And it remained the whole man. Throughout his career everything he did was directly subordinated to certain ideas, some fixed, some changing, which he reached through independent thought. Thus, when he stood as a Liberal candidate, it was not because he was converted to Liberalism (he prided himself on getting through his campaign without once mentioning Mr. Gladstone); and when, later, he joined the Conservatives, it was not because he had been converted to Conservatism. Everything he did, whether it met with approval or disapproval from the world, was done because he thought it the right thing to do.

Which is to say that approval and disapproval were irrelevant. When, for example, Mr. Winston Churchill one day praised the great statesman and the next day fell to jeering at 'this disconsolate proconsul', he was merely expressing Churchillian praise and blame for actions the causes and motives of which he could not even faintly comprehend.

Nevertheless, with Goschen, the young Milner for the first and last time in his life threw himself into the game of political manœuvre with his habitual large enjoyment. Gladstone had just split the Liberals on the Irish Home Rule issue, and Milner, curiously and instinctively anticipating the great passion of his life, found himself all of a sudden one of the most active and determined members of the Liberal-Unionist committee. His attitude to the Home Rule struggle at this time was so characteristic of his attitude towards the great questions of his maturity that it is worth bringing out: the attitude of a man who decides on the desirability of a certain course of action, not because it promises perfection, but because, in the given circumstances, it appears to him the least harmful course of action, and who, once the decision is taken, throws himself into the struggle unhesitatingly and without repining. In October, after the 1886 General Election, he went to Ireland to see the country for himself, and in a letter to his chief wrote as follows:

And all the time the people in Ireland who know most and care most for their country are praying for 'a little wholesome neglect'. If only the House of Commons could be shut up for ten years—the other organs of Government going on as usual—what a transformation scene we should witness in poor politician-ridden Ireland, without ourselves, perhaps, being much the worse. . . ! I can only say that I am profoundly thankful that by the goodness of Providence, and your influence, I was saved from taking the Gladstonian side in the late struggle. All my natural leanings were to Home Rule, and, in the far future, I still think it may be the best, or the only constitution for Ireland; but, under present circumstances, I am sure it would have meant a most fearful disaster. . . . As far as I can see ahead, I have no hesitation in saying that I am, for all practical purposes, a Tory. I don't mean, however, to question for a moment the wisdom, nay, the absolute necessity, of keeping up the Liberal Unionist party, for the time at least, as a separate organisation. . . .

So, time and again throughout his life, he was to show the rare gift in a man of action of seeing all sides of the question—or, to look at it from another angle, the rare gift in a serious thinker of acting with decision. Before that year was out he was acting again, this time prompting his chief with all the energy at his command, to an action which was not only to commit the Liberal Unionists to a coalition with Lord Salisbury and make Goschen himself Chancellor of the Exchequer, but also, as a by-product, to break the career of Lord Randolph Churchill.

For some time Lord Randolph Churchill, as Chancellor of the Exchequer, had been making the life of his own Party leader extremely difficult by presuming on his own indispensability and lending his support to the Opposition in a variety of ways. Now, soon after the Home Rule election, he developed a new quarrel with his fellow Ministers about the Service estimates, which he wanted severely reduced. Quite unscrupulously he held the Prime Minister up to ransom by sending in his resignation, taking it for granted that this would be refused: the disagreement was not conceivably serious enough to justify the jeopardising of his career; but Churchill had been getting his own way in other matters and he proposed to continue doing so. Unfortunately for him, in his own words, he 'forgot Goschen', broken with the Liberals and much readier than he guessed to join the Conservatives. To his extreme surprise, Lord Salisbury accepted his resignation, installed Goschen as Chancellor of the Exchequer with W. H. Smith as Leader of the House, and Lord Randolph Churchill never saw office again.

I have only just seen *The Times* with the tremendous news of Randolph's resignation [Milner at once wrote off to his chief], and it has struck me all of a heap, to use a vulgar phrase. It is hard to imagine any adequate justification for him, and his desertion at so critical a moment is, I cannot help thinking, a great blow to the Government and the country. The Gladstonians will regain heart, the Radical Unionists will be less likely to stick to the Ministry, and the Irish and foreign countries will lose their salutary belief in the stability of the Government. Knowing all this, as he must know it, he is surely guilty of unpardonable egoism in imperilling the whole prospects of his country and his party rather than abate anything of his extreme self-will.

The only good I can see out of this catastrophe is that the Government may be forced to have recourse to you. . . .

And three days later he was writing of the crisis:

I am the last person to underrate its gravity, but there is a compensating advantage in the more natural arrangement of parties, to which it ought to give rise. Randolph gone—there is no substantial difference between moderate Liberals, like yourself and Hartington, and progressive Conservatives. Assuming, as I think one may, that your and Hartington's only thought will be how best to keep the Ministry in office, every hour's reflection confirms the opinion that the best course of all would be for you to join them and Hartington to continue to lead a friendly band of Liberal Unionists, the next best for Hartington and you both to join them, the worst of all— but that most likely to be adopted—for them to go on as they are. I can't say how strongly I wish for their sake, the country's sake, and your sake, that the first solution should be adopted. It seems as if the crisis, for which you have long been holding yourself in reserve, had actually come.

And three days later again, on December 29th, 1886: '. . . I will only say, that I remain impenitently of opinion, of deep conviction, rather, that your place is with the army that wants a leader, rather than with the leaders who want an army.'

When Goschen acted as Milner hoped and urged, accepting office as Chancellor of the Exchequer in Randolph Churchill's place, Milner went with him as his Official Private Secretary.

It seemed worth quoting extensively from those three letters, written in the heat of a long-forgotten political crisis, because they offer us the first glimpse of Milner in action on the large stage. And in this action we see unmistakably the born statesman with a gift for political manœuvre. One of the differences between the statesman and the political careerist lies, precisely, in their attitude to manœuvre and intrigue. The careerist tacks and intrigues for his own personal ends; the statesman makes use of the intrigues of others, as the sailor uses wind and tide and current, to help him to a predetermined landfall. The doctrinaire idealist tries to behave, and often succeeds disastrously enough, as though there were no such things as winds and tides and currents.

In that short correspondence, dealing with a single narrow issue, we can see the whole of Milner's future development. The man who, at thirty-two, and only lately arrived behind the political scene, could, in a moment of general excitement and consternation and furious speculation, size up the issue, immediately decide on the proper course of action for the main actors, and urge it without the least qualification or ambiguity on his chief, was going to be drawn irresistibly into the heart of events. He would not be happy until he was in a position to make his opinions effective on a national scale. On the other hand, those were not the words of a man who associated the cause of an idea with his own public exaltation. They were the words of a man with a genius for managing who, provided he was given a full-sized job to do and a free hand in organising it, cared not at all whether it earned him popular fame. That reading is borne out by what followed. The man who wanted to shine in the eyes of the world, having stretched his wings to such effect, would have launched forthwith into a political career. Milner did not. He had already given up the idea of Parliament, at least for the time being, and for the next ten years he served anonymously—anonymously, that is, as far as the general public was concerned, but with ever-increasing reputation among the political leaders of the day. After two years with Goschen he went to Cairo as Financial Under-Secretary to the Government of Egypt. Three years later, at thirty-eight, and with his character fully formed, he came back to be Chairman of the Board of Inland Revenue, where he found the work 'hard, important, and boring', and where he was responsible for the introduction of Death Duties as a source of revenue (in later years he was to regard with horror the way in which this innocent and harmless device had been extended to change the whole structure of society). Here, too, he had every opportunity for giving full play to his delight in figures and the effortless untangling of mathematical muddles: for him figures had a life of their own. In dealing with statistics of every kind the bleak little groups of integers each possessed its own unique character, never to be forgotten. Thus, later, as an administrator, he would present a closely argued financial case without once referring to a note.

Such were his talents, however, that this particular gift, in itself sufficient to make for most men a first-class career, was quite incidental to the qualities which caused him to be singled out for high office. And when after five years at Somerset House, at forty-three, he was appointed Governor of Cape Colony and High Commissioner for South Africa, after refusing an under-secretaryship in the Salisbury Government, it was not because he was good at figures: he was appointed for his character and vision. It was the most formidable moment, since the American War of Independence, in the history of the British Empire, and the post which Milner accepted was the most vulnerable, thankless, and important in the realm.

At that time he had no enemies (these were yet to come), and the tremendous send-off was shared in by the leaders of all political parties without a touch of malice. Nobody wanted to see him fail. He had earned for himself the reputation of a first-class administrator and a natural statesman, distinguished by a combination of firmness, tact, common sense, and vision—qualities too often mutually exclusive, but here united in a single man whom even the most case-hardened political climber could afford to admire because of his disinterest in the coveted prizes of office.

'There is no case of the selection of a young and comparatively untried man for high and responsible work which has reflected more honour upon the insight and foresight of a Minister, and been more fruitful of advantage to the public service itself.' Thus Mr. Asquith, for the Opposition, speaking of Milner's career at the banquet given in his honour before he left for South Africa.

Nor was Asquith alone:

The appointment [wrote Sir Edward Grey] is the greatest compliment the Government could pay you, for the post is just now the most difficult and important at their disposal; and the work will be so interesting that it is not worth while for your friends to ask how far it will be agreeable. . . . The difficulties are enough to put any man upon his mettle and you must feel braced and stimulated, but perhaps a little grim at the prospect. Be that as it may, what I really want to say is that there are very few men indeed in whom I should feel so much, and no one in whom I should feel more confidence than in you in such a place and that this will be a very great help to me, if it comes to voting in the House of Commons.

This was the send-off of the future leaders of that Party which was later to drag Milner's name in the mud.

Chapter Five

THE WHITE MAN'S BURDEN

Egypt, of course, had made him and developed in him
the passion of his life. Under Lord Cromer he was able to
see the British Imperial idea at its highest and most free;
and the immense personal success of Cromer may very well have
blinded him a little to the difficulties in the way of the full and
more general realisation of this idea. In his early South African
days he himself left no formal record of his aims; and, apart from
his book, *England in Egypt*, he wrote and said little about the
Imperial attitude in general until after his return from South
Africa. But, in fact, disconnected remarks and a few passages
from *England in Egypt* are quite enough to show that from the
beginning in South Africa he was thinking clearly and strongly
along the lines he was later to organise into a highly developed
creed. He believed, of course, in the White Man's Burden. . . .
'It is not only, or principally, upon what Englishmen do for
Egypt that the case for England rests. It is upon what England
is helping the Egyptians to do for themselves. British influence is
not exercised to impose an uncongenial foreign system upon a
reluctant people. It is a force making for the triumph of the
simplest ideas of honesty, humanity, and justice, to the value of
which the Egyptians are just as much alive as anybody else. . . .'
He held this belief with sombre passion. And his whole tenure of
South Africa was dominated by his concern for the native population. It is characteristic that from the outset, when another man
would have been wholly wrapped up in the details of the quarrel
between the English and the Boers, with the rights of the British
settlers in the Transvaal, he was able to recognise the native
problem as the heart and crux of the South African problem as a
whole—as, in fact, it remains to this day. He had his first direct

experience of it during the Jubilee celebrations, when Mrs. Hanbury-Williams, who acted as hostess at Government House, presented with bouquets by a small white girl and a small black girl, kissed them both impartially, causing a storm of protest.

In one respect, however, I must vindicate my friends of the Press [Milner wrote to Canon Glazebrook some months after this]. You say that they have reported nothing except that Mrs. Hanbury-Williams kissed a black child as well as a white one. But that is really the most important thing that has happened since I came here —at least it has excited the greatest amount of general public interest and controversy. I think she was right. Most white people in South Africa think she was wrong. There you have the great S. African problem posed at once. It is the Native question. The Anglo-Dutch friction is bad enough. But it is child's play compared with the antagonism of White and Black. That the white man must rule is clear—but *How?* That is the point, where my views and those of most Englishmen differ radically from those of most Colonists. And this, and not the Dutch business, is the subject with respect to which I foresee the greatest difficulty.

By 'the Dutch business' he meant, primarily, the conflict about the status of British settlers in the Transvaal, who were denied by Kruger's government the rights of free citizens. But, in fact, a main ingredient of 'the Dutch business' was, precisely, the Native question. While Milner had no hesitation in castigating his own countrymen for what he considered their improper treatment of natives, he knew very well that Dutch opposition to any attempt to raise the blacks to a higher level of civilisation was fanatical and implacable, and had a great deal to do with their attitude towards the British Government.

If ever a man had every excuse for shelving vast, general, and apparently insoluble problems while he concentrated on the immediate quarrel of the moment, it was Milner in 1897. There is no better way not only to illuminate the breadth of his character but also to put the whole struggle with the Boers into perspective— the perspective in which he himself constantly saw it—than to consider his views on the colour question as elaborated at the very outset of his African career. They occur in a letter to Mr. Asquith, and, apart from its intrinsic interest and value, it is a sidelight on Milner's extraordinary conscientiousness and his fierce determination to spare himself no effort to foster a united policy towards Imperial affairs:

I have just been reading with great interest . . . the substance of a speech . . . in which you dealt largely with our S. African difficulties. With your great two principles that (1) we should 'seek to restore the good relations between the Dutch and the English', and (2) we should 'secure for the Natives, particularly in that part of Africa called Rhodesia, adequate and sufficient protection against oppression and wrong', I most cordially agree, with this reservation, that I don't quite see the ground for your 'particularly'. It seems to me, we are equally bound to secure the good treatment of the natives in the Transvaal, where we specially and most solemnly promised them protection when we gave back the country to the Boers, and inserted the provision in the Convention giving us the fullest right to intervene on their behalf. This, however, though an important point, is not the particular point, which I want to make in this letter. What I am so anxious that you and other English Statesmen, especially Liberal Statesmen, should understand is that object No. 2 is the principal obstacle to the attainment of object No. 1, is, and always has been. . . . I should feel quite confident of being able to get over the Dutch-English difficulty if it were not so horribly complicated by the Native question. . . . Rhodesia is a case in point. The blacks have been scandalously used. Even now, though *there is great amendment*, and though the position of the black man in Rhodesia is now probably more hopeful than in any part of South Africa not under direct imperial control, except Natal, I am not at all confident that many bad things will not happen. I am doing my best, in fact there is nothing out here which I consider so important or so difficult—but I have to walk with extreme caution, for nothing is more certain than that if the Imperial Government *were to be seen taking a strong line* against the Company [Rhodesia] for the protection of the blacks, the whole of Dutch opinion in South Africa would swing round to the side of the Company and the bulk of—not the whole of—British Colonial opinion would go with it. . . You have, therefore, this singular situation, that you might unite Dutch and English by protecting the black man, but you would unite them against yourself and your policy of protection. There is the whole *crux* of the S. African position. . . .

It is easier for us today not only to appreciate the very real meaning of the White Man's Burden, that phrase which for half a century degraded the Imperialist idea to a music-hall joke, but also to estimate the variable fitness of different races of white men to carry it. This was, as Milner saw, the nub of the South African problem—a fact which was obscured and confused by the spectacular confusion of the South African war. It is impossible to understand how the war came about or to appreciate Milner's own part in it, or to see in perspective the subsequent development of South African history, without constant reference to that deadly reef upon which British influence in South Africa is at this moment foundering. Milner believed with all the deep passion of which he was capable that England was responsible for the protection of the native population of South Africa. He fought for the natives and against all those who sought to exploit them, including the British element. And only when we consider the specific attitude of the Boers towards the natives under their rule, an attitude perfectly reflected today in the official attitude of the Cape Town Government, does it become possible to understand Milner's attitude to the question of war and peace.

What was it, Lady Oxford was to speculate in her diary, 'that had produced the violence in his mind?' She had just come from meeting Milner in the most bitter moment of his life, when, at the instance of her own friends and others, he had been censured in the Commons and publicly pilloried as a monster of reaction. She was astonished by his gentleness, his lack of rancour, the way in which, far from glowering at his enemies, he sought to put them at their ease. She simply could not understand how a man so evidently upright, just and generous should have yielded himself to reactionary policies. One cause of what Lady Oxford called the violence in his mind was, precisely, his determination to preserve the African natives from utter exploitation by Briton or Boer, and his conviction that, as far as the Boers went, they could probably never be restrained by anything but force— since, by denying the franchise to British settlers, they were blocking the only peaceful path to a more liberal form of government in the Transvaal. Another cause was his conviction that in an imperfect world, the British character had elements worthy of preservation and development; and this, in a world ruled by force, called for the occasional unequivocal display of force. Nobody, as we shall see, could have been more conscious than Milner of the shortcomings of the British. But on the whole, and in his more buoyant periods, he believed that when it came to the pinch they had achieved a maturity of outlook and a decency of aspiration which, combined, made them the most likely leaders in an imperfect world. In the nature of things, somebody was going to lead: therefore it had better be Britain. If Britain refused that fence, others, less fitted for any kind of leadership, or trusteeship, or whatever, would rush it. For Britain to lead, however—and this, among other things, involved filling the formidable power-vacua produced by the uneven material development of the world —she had to be strong. The only way to maintain the requisite strength was to develop the backward areas whose protection depended on that strength. It was as simple as that. Because it was so simple, because it was so overpoweringly obvious, Milner took it too much for granted. His tragedy was that he took it for granted that others saw it too.

And thus it is that the more his speeches and writings are studied, the clearer it becomes that he was profoundly at cross-purposes with most of his contemporaries. These, because the British were not perfect, because they were beginning to doubt the bland, unjustified assumptions of the past, were abandoning the small hard fact of relative good for the chimera of absolute virtue. They were preparing the day when a President of America should offer to save the world from Communism precisely by developing the backward areas of this planet. But the backward areas of President Truman's fourth point were, in Milner's day, British possessions or dependencies. And the origin of all Milner's thought and action is to be found in one simple concern: the survival of Britain and her Empire in an always competitive and frequently hostile world. The purpose of all his thought and action was first to ensure that survival and then to see that Britain used her power for the best in an imperfect world. To this end he advocated not only obvious policies, such as the development of sufficient armed strength to enable the country to hold its own, but also the most far-reaching social reforms as part of a general policy for improving the stamina and the decency of the British people.

Since it is the first duty of a national statesman to work for his country's survival, there should be nothing peculiar about Milner's attitude. But, in fact, it was unusual in this country. People then took survival for granted and, in their desire for a perfect world, played fast and loose with the impossible. A moment's reflection will show that the first consideration of the majority of British statesmen during the past half-century has been a quiet life at any cost. At its best, this attitude has implied a striving for the comfort and concord of the world in general and the British people in particular; at its worst it has reflected the politician's natural craving for an infinite and untroubled term of office. More often than not, these motives have been mixed. Almost invariably, too, the idea of a quiet life has been confused with the idea of peace.

This confusion is not new; but it is only during the present century that it has threatened the very existence of civilisation, if not of the inhabited world. The desire for a quiet life is immemorial, and through the centuries it has been frustrated and confounded by the terms of life itself. The more ardently it is sought for its own sake, the more it recedes. The pursuit of cosiness ends with a bang, not a whimper. For the world is not a cosy place, and the longer it is held at arm's length the harsher will be its impact when at last it breaks through the plush or chromium defences. Peace, on the other hand, is a technical term for a technical condition. If it means anything at all in the international context it means an absence of war, which itself is a technical term (and, indeed, how narrowly technical these two terms, war and peace, have always been, is clearly demonstrated today when the so-called 'cold war' between the Communists and the rest has carried the lethal potentialities of technical non-belligerence to something like their logical conclusion, bringing the world to a state which, according to traditional reckoning, is neither war nor peace). Peace, peace between nations, as alien to the terms of life as cosiness, can in fact be secured. But it can be secured only by the use of force. It cannot, in a word, be bought: it can only be imposed—an unnatural condition imposed by natural means, and at the cost of a quiet life.

Only the strong, among those who desire peace, are in a position to impose it. Thus even if it is argued that the first duty of a modern statesman is to strive for universal peace, in practice this comes to the duty of making his country strong in order to impose its will for peace on others who lack that will. The most straightforward way of doing this in an imperfect world is to weaken one's enemies by sustaining one's friends. The traditional British policy, which is very much older than Munich, is to seek to buy peace by appeasing the enemy at the expense of friends.

This policy when exposed in black and white will not bear scrutiny. It has to be disguised by the pretence that the enemy is not really an enemy at all—or, more actually, by magnifying the justness of the enemy's claims while deprecating one's own position—and one's friends'. And this, in fact, is what happens. Milner, at the turn of the century, was most acutely conscious of it, as no English statesman ever had been. His whole life was devoted to the survival of Britain and the Empire at a time when not only the intellectuals but also many politicians were actively anti-Imperialist, when, indeed, Imperialism was equated with jingoism as a term of abuse.

We are discussing Milner, not the British character; and this is no place to analyse the many separate strands which went to the weaving of the rope designed expressly for the attempted suicide of this extraordinary race. But it is necessary to point out that Milner's own attitude had its blindness. He saw, as nobody saw, the situation with its latent crisis. He was perfectly aware that Great Britain alone could not stand up as an independent power. The days when, unable to feed herself from her own resources, she could yet maintain a relatively high standard of living by selling her manufactured goods, were passing, with the growth of industry everywhere. To him it was plain as a pike-staff that the Empire, held together and developed, could indeed become self-supporting and at the same time strong for peace. He also saw this supreme and never recurring opportunity being frittered away by the lack of imagination and timidity—the desire for a quiet life—of the people at home. And against all this he protested with all his might in words and action. But what he did not see—and this was a serious blindness—was the full complexity and muddle of the motives behind the drift towards abdication. It was serious because he was thus unable to allow for these motives and frame his attack accordingly. He overlooked the whole muddle, glorious or inane, of aspiration towards a guilt-free existence, which has conditioned all characteristically British behaviour for the past half-century. He missed in its entirety the Puritan conscience. And because in so many of his speeches and his actions he never allowed for this, all too often he goaded it into stiffer opposition and got himself labelled as a stiff-necked chauvinist, foreign to liberal ideas.

He was temperamentally incapable of entertaining the sentimental guilt-consciousness the presence of which in the British character has had so many fatal consequences, but which may, if it is not too late, still prove a redeeming virtue. It is this fact which partly vitiated his own tremendous efforts and which made one of the most advanced thinkers of his time come to be regarded as a rigid reactionary by many Englishmen who lagged far behind him in enlightenment. If Milner threw himself into a plan for reform, for the improvement of the lot of the unfortunate, he did so because the plan seemed to him reasonable and right. But the twentieth-century humanitarianism, which saw him as a monster, owed its origins far less to an exact appreciation of right and wrong, of the practical and the unpractical, than to an impulsive revulsion against past wrongs which had, somehow, to be atoned for. The British Empire had to go because many crimes had been committed in its name. Milner, if he had grasped this attitude at all, would have seen it as irrelevant. He was responsible for his own sins, but not for the sins of his fathers—which in any case could not be atoned for by the simple and effortless process of undoing their work. One might as well say that the whole world should commit suicide because of original sin.

This attitude, unstated (for the simple reason that Milner was unaware of it), profoundly affronted the sentimental humanitarianism of his day. The blindness was not in the attitude, which must have been the attitude of any clear thinker, but in Milner's unawareness of it, which caused him to misdirect his attack. He thought he was attacking laziness, shiftiness, *laissez-faire* opportunism, when in fact he was attacking what may for convenience be labelled the liberal conscience, which acted as a screen for all these shortcomings, and others too, but which was also inseparably mixed with another aspect of the British character, the passion for fair play. For it is no accident that in the eyes of the world England should be seen almost in the same breath as both perfidious Albion and the fountain-head of fair play. Perfidious Albion we certainly are, because our love of justice, colliding with our more human attributes, such as an eye to the main chance and a longing for a quiet life, embroils us in situations which we are not prepared to see through. We are not, in a word, prepared to pay the price of our ideals when the price is high, or until, as in war, we are fairly driven to it in sheer self-defence. On the other hand, the ideals exist, and when the price is not too high, we pursue them with enthusiasm. The individual, moreover, is prepared to pay higher for his ideals as an individual than the nation is prepared to pay as a nation. And so we have the paradox of the Englishman whose word is as good as his bond in his capacity of private citizen becoming a hypocrite in his capacity of public citizen. The downfall is all the greater because the aim has been so high. Nobody expects decent public behaviour from a German, because the German takes no stock in decency. The Englishman, on the contrary, talks a good deal about decency, out of decency aims higher than he should—with what results we all know. Out of decency, too, the Englishman deplores his grandfather's sins and tries to atone for them cheaply by betraying his grandfather's friends. More than this, he frequently deplores his own sins and equally blithely betrays his own friends who helped him commit them. Thus at Munich the British, feeling guilty about Versailles, cheerfully sacrificed not only their own interests but also the interests of their friends and supporters in a one-sided attempt to appease the enemy.

Thus in South Africa, the exponents of the liberal conscience were outraged by the apparent repetition of the worst incidents of British Empire building. They thought of India. They were genuinely horrified by the prospect of a war with a lot of truculent but apparently honest Dutch farmers for the sake, as it seemed to them, of the scallywag plutocrats of the Rand—a predatory raid on an inoffensive people by gold-crazed adventurers. They lacked the mental equipment to sit back and work out their attitude in terms of life. Life should be perfect. The Boer War was not perfect. Therefore it must be opposed.

This attitude, almost unbelievably silly in our present age, when we have been sharply reminded of the realities of life by two waves of German aggression, by Pearl Harbour, and by the bleak Darwinism of the Kremlin, did not seem silly to countless decent Englishmen at the turn of the century, a period in which everything was moving forward to brightness and light, and a little England, secure behind the Channel and doling out manufactured articles to an insatiable world in exchange for raw materials and a great variety of food, had only to divest herself of all the gains of past greed to sit smugly on top of the world as the shining exemplar of justice on earth. To those who were accustomed to thinking in radical terms, to Milner, for example, it seemed insufferably silly even then—so silly that it could not be believed. In this he was born very much before his time. For instead of exposing the silliness for what it was, his mind, intent on reality, saw it as no more than a manifestation of unstable popular sentiment deliberately exploited by Liberal politicians for their own ends. Heaven knows, there was some truth in this. But the popular sentiment existed, as a fact; and the Liberal politicians, being first and foremost Englishmen, did not so much cynically exploit it in full knowledge of what they were doing as drift with it, allowing it to form their policies. So Milner, proceeding on his set course, was vulnerable.

But if he was vulnerable, he was also magnificent. Although his diagnosis was not correct, he was at least aware of the disease, and he fought it unremittingly. The battle was on two fronts. It was waged on behalf of the greater good, as he saw it, against the greater evil; and it was waged against those who, overcome by the realisation of the elementary fact that there was bad also on their side and good also on the other side, allowed themselves to be deflected from any recognisable purpose, leaving such crudities to those with evil intent. The disease was deep. In a passage to which we shall later return, a sympathetic historian lamenting Milner's shortcomings as a diplomat, wrote of him: 'Slow to make up his mind, he never wavered once he had made it up and was apt to see wrong-headedness and even moral obliquity in those who differed from him.' Those words were written in 1942 when civilisation was falling into dust precisely because for too long too many Englishmen had been too unsure of themselves, or, worse, too puffed-up with their own fair-mindedness, *not* to see 'wrong-headedness and even moral obliquity' in their opponents. Increasingly aware of our own immense hypocrisies and treacheries, caught up by the sense of guilt and harassed by the buffetings of a new, unpractised, unbalanced conscience, we found ourselves unable to condemn the sins of others. Blinded by the mote in our own eye we failed to see the beam in the eye of our neighbour. With what results. . . .

There is no doubt at all that Milner did in fact sometimes exaggerate the conscious ill-will of his opponents. It was the reaction of a man accustomed to thinking straight and seeing clearly, who found it impossible to fathom the depths of intellectual squalor in which most of us quite cheerfully live out our days. It was a limitation on his part, and a limitation which had unfortunate consequences, as we shall later see. But it is also true that in the Boer attitude he did see wrong-headedness and moral obliquity, and it was precisely that wrong-headedness and moral obliquity which so many of us see today in the policies of Dr. Malan. It is not enough for us to say that the problem of black and white in South Africa is a difficult one: we live in a difficult world. It is not enough for us to say that we ourselves are miserable sinners: that is a platitude, not an original proposition. Yet this was precisely the attitude which Milner had to face—the abdication of all responsibility, and the refusal to choose a course of clear-cut action and stick to it because no course of action was perfect, because the country owed its strength to past sins as much as to past virtues, and because the sins of others had extenuating circumstances. Milner was aware of all this: he was also aware of its irrelevance. Thirty years later he was equally aware that the Treaty of Versailles was an imperfect treaty—and of the irrelevance of that. Forty years later he would have been equally aware that we had behaved badly to the Bolsheviks in the past—and of its irrelevance. He would have regarded both Hitler and Stalin as guilty of 'wrong-headedness and even of moral obliquity'. We are told that to understand is to forgive. But who says we can understand?

PART TWO

STATESMAN AND PROCONSUL

Chapter Six

THE MAKING OF A MYTH

S OUTH AFRICA WAS not only the test of Milner's character, ability, and wisdom: it was also the arena in which, for good or ill, he earned his public reputation. Against that obscure and treacherous background he won his greatest triumphs and suffered his profoundest disappointments. For nearly half a century, as 'the man who made the Boer War', he has been denied a true appreciation of his qualities because of his association with an episode which, for a number of interesting reasons, was chosen to symbolise everything disreputable in the history of the British Empire. It is not the purpose of this study to dwell for its own sake on the South African War, but without some kind of an appreciation of the causes of that war it is impossible to understand the sort of man that Milner was: conversely, a knowledge of the sort of man he was calls at once for a fairly radical revision of the popular idea of that war.

Seeing the present state of the world, and the continued dominion, despite the cloudy aspirations of the millions, of what is tautologically called power politics, it will hardly be disputed that the idea of the Boer War as a uniquely shameful lapse into unnatural barbarism was a wrong idea. In view of the collapse of the Pax Britannica and the chaos that has succeeded it— a chaos to which few of us see an end—the myth of the South African war as an iniquitous episode in the iniquitous history of an iniquitous nation is seen not only to be false in itself, but also catastrophic in its consequences. For what, in the first decades of this present century did most of us know of human wickedness or the relativity of human virtue? 'The better is the enemy of the good' was one of Milner's favourite tags, which he never tired of quoting. Translated into terms of empires it could read today: Where the District Officer walks out, the Commissar walks in.

It is worth remembering that the controversy about the Boer War did not develop its full heat until it was over. Certainly while the war was on there was a strong pro-Boer movement in this country; but it was never powerful enough to have more than a delaying effect on the country's policy. On the other hand, the unhappy interlude of the so-called rebellion, when the British, with their concentration camps for women and their burning of defenceless farms, gave the world the first hint of what long-repressed savagery was capable of when it broke through the veneer of nineteenth-century civilisation—this interlude marked the victory of popular feeling over the restraint of the leaders, who, when the public came to its senses, were condemned for the iniquities they had stubbornly resisted.

The two main strands in pro-Boer feeling were on the one hand the characteristic and instinctive sympathy of the ordinary Englishman for the under-dog, aggravated by shame, and, on the other, the highly articulate Left-wing pedantry, which saw in the struggle a classical example of the predatory advance of uncontrolled and unscrupulous big business. It was not until after the war that these two strands, woven into a national conscience largely awakened by the brutalities of the war, became the rope with which the British Empire was to hang itself. In other words, during his first South African years Milner was not opposed for what he did. But what he did, with the full support of the country, was destined to fill the country with a sentimental revulsion against its own past behaviour which was to bring down first the man charged to represent its interests and, later, the country itself, as a great power in a world of great powers. Milner, of course, was not conscious of this: it is to be doubted whether he was ever fully aware of the forces at work in the early years of the century. Nor, for that matter, were the politicians who, for party advantage, invited the first impact of enfranchised mass opinion on the conduct of foreign and imperial affairs.

The South African War was the division between two ages, and the boundary was not clear. It had its origins in the past, in the days when foreign and imperial policy was conducted in comparative obscurity and with instinctive realism by traditional rulers who understood each other's thoughts and motives and spoke the same language. At the same time it marked the coming of age of an epoch of popular nationalism, born in Paris a hundred years before, which, combining with the revolutionary spirit, was to throw up a succession of nationalist leaders, usually of humble origin, and nearly always without a word or a thought in common with each other. A simultaneous phenomenon, and strongly contributory to the spirit of revolutionary nationalism in its own despite, was the rise of finance capital, as exemplified in South Africa by the financiers of the Transvaal. Thus, in a limited sense, it could be said that the Boer War was the first Marxist war. But it did not look like that at the time. And one of the few men who had an inkling of this aspect of the affair was Milner himself, who, nearly twenty years earlier, had lectured on Karl Marx (then still living in Finchley) to a world which had not yet heard of him.

It was also the last legalistic war. After that, nations which wanted more room or more wealth were to go to war if they felt they could win. But the British in South Africa invoked the legal sanctions of an already foreign age. The official position has been admirably summed up by Mr. Headlam:

> The right of Great Britain to the Cape Colony was, in fact, the right of conquest, capitulation, cession, purchase, occupation, and development. Her title-deed was the Convention of August 13, 1814. Throughout the greater part of the Napoleonic Wars she had been at war with Holland. On January 28, 1806, for the second time a British expedition wrested the Cape from the Dutch. At the Peace Settlement in 1814, Great Britain restored to the Netherlands (Holland and Belgium) the East Indies and all the Dutch Colonies she had captured during the war, except the Cape of Good Hope and what is now British Guiana. These she retained, paying in consideration thereof £6,000,000 sterling. With her new acquisition, vital to her as a half-way house to India, she inherited a legacy of prolonged misrule and financial confusion left by the bankrupt Dutch East India Company. In 1805, after a century and a half of Dutch rule, the white civil population of the Cape Colony numbered only 26,000, and this included many English, Germans and French Huguenots, as well as Dutch and half-castes. After seventy years of British administration, it had risen to nearly a quarter of a million,

yielding a revenue of £4,000,000, in spite of Boer migrations and the settlement of many Dutch and English colonists in Natal and the North.

The right of the British to the Cape was not officially disputed by the Boers of the South African Republic and their Afrikander supporters in the Orange Free State, in Natal, and in Cape Colony itself: the war when it came was fought on quite other grounds. But the behaviour of Kruger's government was for many years conditioned by the smouldering determination of the Dutch to push the British out of South Africa altogether, so that all the colonies could be united into a single federated Dutch Republic: *Afrika voor de Afrikaners.* This credo was proclaimed in 1881 after Majuba Hill, and the Boers were exhorted to look to their arms against the day when 'the time is ripe for asserting the nation's rights and being rid of English thraldom'. That the British Government of the day was largely to blame for this state of mind is undeniable. When the Boers had trekked away to the north to escape from British sovereignty after the cession of Cape Colony, they had crossed the Vaal and founded the republic of the Transvaal, which stagnated on pastoral lines until the discovery of immense mineral wealth and the consequent influx of foreign settlers, largely British, to exploit it. In 1877, advised by many influential Boers, the British Government formally annexed the Transvaal, an action which could only have been justified by the determination and ability to hold it and develop it along enlightened lines. But when three years later the Boers revolted and, in 1881, inflicted on the British forces the disaster of Majuba Hill, London tamely capitulated. Lacking the necessary ruthlessness to make good the British title by force, it sought a compromise which contained the germs of catastrophe: the Boers were granted their full independence except in foreign affairs, which were to remain under British supervision. And from that time onwards the Boers were quite clear in their minds that Britain would always knuckle under to a show of force, and that sooner or later successful revolt would spread to Cape Colony itself. To this end, Kruger's government steadily and stealthily set about building up its military strength.

It was this illusion that the British would always give way which Milner saw as the key to the whole situation. It was an illusion strengthened by the time he arrived by the consequences of the Jameson Raid. And it was an illusion which could only be dispelled by an unambiguous display of determination and might on the part of the British Government, which, however, seemed, as so often, content to utter stern pronouncements without providing itself with the means to make good its words.

There was nothing, officially, that could be said about the arming of the Boers with the latest products of the Continental arsenals: this was done secretly. But Milner was acutely conscious of it from the beginning of his tour, and the consideration that rifles, machine-guns, field artillery, and ammunition in large quantities were being convoyed across the territory for which he was responsible into the Transvaal profoundly influenced words and actions which, on the face of it, might have seemed untowardly rigorous and severe. His official quarrel was centred not on the Boer preparations to drive the British into the sea, but on their treatment of British subjects who had settled in the Transvaal, the Uitlanders, looking for gold and diamonds among the agrarian Boers. These certainly included plenty of bad characters, the riff-raff of every gold rush; and the methods employed by the British business men engaged in exploiting the gold were often characteristic of capitalism in its most dismal manifestations. But the Boers had nothing against exploitation as such, provided they grew wealthy on it. They welcomed the prosperity of the new towns, and were only concerned with seeing that the despised Uitlander was not allowed a voice in the government of their republic. What made them hate the English was, above all, the British attitude towards the native question. The Boers were determined to be free to exploit the natives in their own way. Of course there were many Englishmen who thought as they did and who regarded the African native as an inferior being, good for nothing but slavery. But this was not the attitude of the more enlightened English or of the British Government. In the Graaf Reinet Manifesto, from which I have already quoted, the following passage occurs: 'Perfidious Albion, for the sake of industrial profit, aims at elevating the natives to equal rank with the whites, in direct conflict with spiritual authority.'

The pastoral picture of the genial, pipe-smoking, easy-going Dutch farmers, pushing up north to escape the contaminating influence of British capitalism, has to be amended a little in the light of the real facts, which were that the Boers had crossed the Vaal River in 1838 to get away from the whole British way of life, above all that aspect of it which found expression in concern for the future of the native Africans. At no stage did the Boers make the least attempt to sabotage the capitalist exploitation of their mineral wealth. They sought only to withhold from the foreign business men any voice in the affairs of the land. And it is worth remembering that in those days it was the house of Dr. Livingstone that was sacked, because he preached the equality of all men. The gold mines, about which later generations of Englishmen were to develop a guilty conscience, were not sacked by the Boers. They were cherished, and they brought the Boer Republic new wealth and the means required to make its bid for a Dutch South Africa. And thus, although from one point of view the war may be seen as the outcome of the inevitable advance of capitalism, from another, at least equally valid, point of view, it arose from a profound difference of attitude towards the native question —a difference which has persisted to this day and outlived all the other quarrels between the British and the Afrikanders until, in the conception of *Apartheid*, it has stretched relations between South Africa and the rest of the Commonwealth almost to breaking point; while the dream of a Dutch Republic stretching from the Limpopo to the Cape is no less active than it was at the time of Majuba Hill and very much closer to fulfilment: a Dutch Republic which would owe its prosperity and security overwhelmingly to British capital, British mildness, and, in its formative years, the power of the Royal Navy.

Chapter Seven

CONFLICT OF CONVICTION

HERE, IN A profound racial opposition, which persists to this day, was the real cause of the South African War. There were other elements in the conflict—the lust for riches and power on the part of individuals and the blind, irresistible advance of modern finance capital. But these, like the individual intrigues of individual politicians, were incidental to the main theme, and therefore fundamentally irrelevant. The main theme was the conflict between the Boer way of life and the British way of life, above all as expressed in native policy. Between these two ways of life there could be no compromise. In other circumstances—had it not been, for example, for the gold of the Rand—these two ways of life might have existed side by side much longer. But sooner or later they would have clashed; and the only escape from war would have been the total submission of the Boers to Britain's demands or the total withdrawal of Britain from South Africa. There could be no question of withdrawal. The British were in Africa legitimately. Within the general framework of imperial expansion, which was not then in question, the British were no more interlopers on the African continent than the Dutch themselves; and the best of the British took their responsibilities to the native population a great deal more seriously than the best of the Dutch. Within the imperial framework, again, Cape Colony was as vital and indispensable to Britain as, for example, the Black Sea coast to Russia or California to the United States. She had to hold it or relapse into the position of a minor power; and in a world full of expanding powers this would have been suicide. Britain had to stay; and it was the deep, considered policy of the Kruger Government to force her out. Milner saw this and was ready to accept the logical conclusion, deeply as he abhorred it. He strove hard to avoid war, so apparently successfully that at times he allowed himself to hope. But always in his mind was the knowledge that unless the Boers made certain concessions war was inevitable. The Boers were in no mood to make concessions. After Majuba Hill relations between British and Dutch grew steadily worse, as the Transvaal Government deliberately put the screws on the British settlers, the Uitlanders. The Jameson Raid of 1896, that ill-considered and reckless attempt to cut the knot, failed completely and ended in the estrangement of Rhodes himself, then Prime Minister of Cape Colony, from his Afrikander colleagues. In the following year the British Cabinet decided that the time had come to invoke the London Convention, which had detailed the rights of the Uitlanders in the Transvaal, and to present the Kruger Government with a Note sufficiently strong to show that they meant business. It was at this moment that Milner went out, a man of forty-three with 'as clear an intellect and as sympathetic an imagination, and, if the need should arise, a power of resolution as tenacious and inflexible as belongs to any man of our acquaintance'. Those were the words of Mr. Asquith, who, in 1897, considered that just these qualities were called for in dealings with the Boers. While to show that this view of the position was not merely a youthful indiscretion on the part of a single Liberal statesman, we may quote the *Daily News*, the Liberal organ which, many years later, was to crown a campaign of vituperation against Milner and all his works with a leading article on his death which read like the indictment of a felon: 'If President Kruger', the *Daily News* wrote in 1897, 'persists in the oppressive and reactionary policy which he has lately emphasised in so many directions, then sooner or later trouble is bound to recur.'

But the quarrel about the Uitlanders was only a symptom of the deeper conflict, and Milner saw this. He also saw, even before he left England, that since the Boers were determined to force the British out of South Africa there was only one way of halting them short of war, and that was by an unambiguous show of resolution backed by material strength. By the time he went out the Boers were hardly troubling to conceal the fact that they were spending the new wealth created for them by the British mines on arms from the Continent to be used one day against the British.

'It is no use talking about what one means and hopes to do', wrote Milner to his old friend, Canon Glazebrook, just before setting out for Cape Town. 'I shall know much better what the chances are when I have been out there for six months. It is an awful job, though I never hesitated when asked to undertake it, and without the favour of the High Gods, it cannot be successfully dealt with. Shall I have that?...'

An awful job it certainly was. He sailed out to it on April 17th, 1897. The Boer ultimatum, which precipitated the war he had for so long seen as inevitable (short of the abdication of Britain's position in South Africa), was delivered on October 9th, 1899. For two and a half years the life of the High Commissioner was to be a struggle on two fronts: with the Boers to prevent war; with the British Government to be ready for war if it should come. Both struggles were foredoomed and forlorn; but this was hardly the failure Milner had in mind when he said he would need the favour of the High Gods. Although he strove with all his might for peace, he did not go out as a missionary for peace. He went out to battle for his country's interest, which, as he conceived it, was also the interest of South Africa and the world. This he upheld. And far from being overcome by a sense of failure when war did break out, he regarded this climacteric simply as the end of a prelude to a much greater task: the building under British auspices of a strong, healthy and pacifically minded South Africa which would play her part as a vital link in the Empire. His failure, as he understood it, came much later. It was the failure to bring round the Home Government to his own way of thinking about the future of South Africa and the Empire as a whole, the failure to achieve his ideal.

In this ideal he believed with sombre passion; and he tackled the problems arising from that belief with a cool and unfaltering realism. On the boat to Cape Town he included Machiavelli in his reading; but it is clear that, when it came to playing high politics, he had nothing to learn from Machiavelli. It has already been suggested that his mind was free in the sense that the mind of the born artist is free: that is to say, he saw, instinctively, every problem and every issue for what it was, clear of preconceptions and conventional associations. He was as free as any man has ever been from the sentimental hypocrisies, or, more accurately, self-deceptions, which fog the minds and blur the actions of the vast majority of his fellow-countrymen. He relied absolutely on the findings of his eye, his instincts, and his brain; and he was never afraid to abide by those findings. He did not put on record his ideas of Utopia. At a time when so many of his contemporaries were convinced that heaven on earth was just round the corner, and rushed towards it with glad cries, he was rather grimly preoccupied, and with a total absorption which made him an antipathetic figure to the light-hearted perfectionists, with the problem of how to induce some sort of order and justice and humanity in a world actively intolerant of these qualities. He took that world as he found it. He was, in a word, wrestling, and almost alone, with the problem which overshadows each one of us today. Most Englishmen of his time thought it no longer existed: it had been solved, they thought, by progress. Progress meant free trade and cotton exports. Lucifer had been vanquished by the spinning-jenny and the forces of darkness by the carbon-arc. Milner did not believe it for a moment.

There is no doubt that his Egyptian experience had given him an insight into the facts of life denied his more insular contemporaries, who would have been all the better for a short course in corruption by the banks of the river of life. There is no doubt, further, that a few months in Cape Town provided him with a deeper experience than any Englishman was to have for the next thirty-five years of the malignant unscrupulousness which a logical and ill-intentioned mind can bring to bear on the destruction of its opponent. But even without Egypt, he knew what the human animal was made of; and what South Africa taught him, above all, was the inadequacy of the British system when it comes to maintaining itself in face of a dedicated enemy.

He arrived at Cape Town in time for the Diamond Jubilee, and the emotional wave of loyalty which swept the Empire gave him a moment's breathing space. But he did not allow himself to be deceived about the realities of the situation; and although for a year he went quietly, trying all the arts of persuasion and holding aloof from the passions of local politics, he knew from the beginning that, sooner or later, if the Kruger Government would not change its ways, war would have to come—unless, also, the whole British position, moral and material, was to be quietly given up. This meant in practice that in all his negotiations he made no attempt to hide his minimum demands. The Boers knew exactly what these were.

It is this situation which makes all criticism of Milner as a diplomat irrelevant and beside the point. This has been a favourite criticism, even among those who have admired him as an administrator. Conflicts of implacable conviction are not amenable to diplomatic treatment. Diplomacy seeks to diminish the area of disagreement, to smooth out misunderstandings, to discover face-saving devices, to achieve compromise in conflicts of ambition. But when all has been done that can be done in this direction and it is found that beneath the surface turmoil a deep cleavage of principle remains, diplomacy is powerless. Its only weapon then is the threat of dire consequences, open or veiled. And this was Milner's position in 1898.

Professor E. A. Walker in his Raleigh Lecture to the British Academy in 1942, from which we have already briefly quoted, unconsciously exposes the whole fallacy. Far from unsympathetic to Milner, he yet believes that had he been a born diplomat, disaster might have been averted.

> All the world knows [he says] that Milner was a splendid administrator, who had given himself up wholly to the services of the State, a man of incredible industry, the mark of whose Reconstruction in South Africa was, as he justly claimed, 'the colossal amount which had been done in the time'. But the world suspected then, and since the publication of the *Milner Papers* knows, that he was less successful as a diplomatist. In those days he was a rigid man, who found it hard to get on terms with the folk whose experience had been different from his own, and his South Africa was lamentably different from anything he had seen in Jowett's Balliol, the offices of the *Pall Mall* in the days of John Morley and W. T. Stead, Lord Cromer's Egypt, or

Sir William Harcourt's Board of Inland Revenue. Slow to make up his mind, he never wavered once he had made it up and was apt to see wrong-headedness and even moral obliquity in those who differed from him. He liked the Afrikander rank-and-file well enough and the patriarchal Boers of the backveld, Nature's gentlemen, still better; but the time came when he found it hard to conceal his loathing of the town-bred lawyer politicians and Reformed clergy who stirred them up by all and every means against his policy and things British.

Milner did not make friends or even contacts easily. No one can say whether the course he took in South Africa would have been different had he possessed that precious gift; certainly the wear and tear on him, and the resentment of his opponents, would have been less in a land where politics were, and are, so much a matter of personal contacts, often over pipes and coffee on the stoep.

Professor Walker goes on, getting closer to the heart of the matter, to make a legitimate point which we have already made in another connection and shall later elaborate: '. . . he despised the parliamentary arts and so failed to tell the electorates, either in South Africa or the United Kingdom, what he was really driving at.'

But this second charge, true in part as it is, has no real connection with the first. When Milner arrived in South Africa 'the town-bred lawyer politicians and Reformed clergy' had it all their own way; and, short of stirring up the Boer population to revolt against Kruger, nothing could have been achieved by any amount of pipe-smoking and coffee-drinking on stoeps—nothing, that is to say, beyond the weakening of his own integrity and the placing of Britain in a false position. Nor, in fact, is the idyllic picture of backveld Boers as 'Nature's gentlemen', as a generalisation, strictly defensible. For, as we have seen, it was the attitude of the backveld Boer to his natives, no less than the attitude of the lawyer politicians to the British settlers, which was a fundamental aspect of the conflict. Pipe-smoking on stoeps, apparently the South African equivalent of political house-parties in Europe, offers every opportunity for resolving conflicts of ambition, which is the proper field for diplomacy. It offers none at all for settling conflicts of conviction. Thus, as an example of the first category of conflict, the then Sir Charles Hardinge was able one August afternoon, on the terrace at Kronberg, over a cigar, to talk the Kaiser into reducing the German naval building programme. But, as an example of the second, no amount of vodka drinking on the terrace at Sochi would enable anyone at all to talk Marshal Stalin out of being a Bolshevik. In so far as Bolshevism is the enemy of our cherished bourgeois way of life, the only thing to do is meet it with strength, and as quietly as possible. In so far as the Bolsheviks are Russians, they will almost certainly balk at a display of strength. But the Boers, with their religious belief in the supremacy of the white man and their quasi-religious belief in the superiority of Afrikanders to all other white men, were not Russians and they did not balk. Milner's job was to give them no excuse for not appreciating the issue and to give them every opportunity to slide out of it. He had no other. In the first he succeeded; but the Boers refused the opportunities.

Thus, strictly, the precise sequence of negotiation, appeal and threat which filled the next two years had, and could have, almost no bearing on the upshot. It was a ritual performance between the leaders of two armies drawn up in battle array. At any time either of the leaders could have given the sign for the retirement and disbanding of his force—but only at the cost of abandoning his whole position and his profoundest convictions. Or, the ritual might have been spun out a little longer. There could be no compromise, however. Milner, when tact was called for, could be tactful to a degree. After all, Asquith himself had praised him for his flexibility. Tact was not here called for. How right Professor Walker was to point out the difference between South Africa of the 'nineties and Balliol, Egypt, the *Pall Mall Gazette*, the Board of Inland Revenue (though he might also have reflected that there were notable differences between all these, and that Milner contrived to adapt himself to them all). But what he missed was the nature of the difference. For in South Africa for all practical purposes Milner was solitary in an enemy camp. The least wavering in his attitude would have been interpreted as indecision; any shallow attempt to gloss over differences in principle by exhibitions of false *camaraderie* would have been a kind of treachery;

and to ingratiate himself with avowed and bitter enemies of the standard he was sent to uphold would have been at best to find an easy solution for himself personally at the expense of the Home Government, at worst to sell the pass. There are moments when all a man can do, without giving himself over entirely to the forces opposed to him, is to stand firm, unequivocally, and hope for the best. Milner's first two years in Africa coincided with one of these moments. He stood firm; and at the same time he knew that it is not enough for a man to stand firm in his own inner consciousness: he must also appear to stand firm.

Chapter Eight

CONCILIATION FROM STRENGTH

THE MISTAKE SO often made in assessing Milner's work as High Commissioner is based on a false premise. His real greatness is to be looked for not in his dealings with the Kruger Government, which, as already suggested, could amount to little more than an elaborate ritual moving to a predetermined end, but in his dealings in South Africa with the anti-Boer extremists on the one hand and the fundamentally disloyal Afrikander and pro-Boer element on the other. These, together with his relations with his masters at the Colonial Office in London, called for statesmanship and diplomatic virtuosity of the rarest kind. Milner supplied them.

Thus the story of the two years which led up to the war was not, as far as Milner was concerned, the story of a dramatic effort to reconcile British and Boer interests (though he did not spare himself in this), but the story of a sustained and protean effort to make sense of British policy, to keep the loyal elements of his own community in step, to frustrate the sedition of the disloyal, and to persuade the Home Government to declare itself so unambiguously that the Kruger Government would know that any attempt to throw out the British by force must fail.

The struggle with the Home Government began even before Milner sailed for Cape Town. The Colonial Office had been busy. Its line, the line that Milner was to champion, was all prepared. The new High Commissioner moved across from Somerset House to find an elaborate draft memorandum to Kruger which recapitulated recent statutory infringements of the London Convention and demanded modifications to a clause in the new Aliens Immigration Law directed against the British settlers in the Transvaal. The tone of this demand had the flavour of an ultimatum. But the British Government at that time was in no position to enforce an ultimatum. Lord Selborne, then Under-Secretary of State for the Colonies, asked Milner for his comments, and Milner replied in a letter which not only showed the clear mind striking hard at its new task but also set the tone for so much that was to happen during the next two years—for the struggle not only with the Boers but also with two of the besetting evils of the British attitude: the inclination of all British Governments to commit themselves to courses which they lack the forces to sustain, and their immemorial incapacity to realise that there are some things which cannot be done on the cheap—among them the maintenance of peace.

On one point I absolutely agree with you [Milner wrote, in his first formal intervention in South African affairs]. I don't think the penultimate and the ante-penultimate paragraphs of that despatch ought to go, unless we have quite clearly made up our minds that, if Law No. 30 is not suspended, we shall go to war. . . . If we are to hold such language without carrying our point in the long run, we shall be terribly discredited. Therefore, in my opinion, we should certainly not hold it, unless we are quite determined to fight on this issue in the last resort. And by determination to fight, I don't mean a vague and abstract resolution, but a tolerably definite plan of action. . . .'

He then went on to give the Colonial Office a classic lesson in how to handle such a situation without yielding an inch of advantage and without prejudice to the employment of stiffer pressure in the future, should the situation warrant it:

Therefore you see that my leaning is towards carrying on the controversy about the Aliens Act in such a manner as will not tie our hands, or compel us to take an irretrievable step with reference to that question alone. . . . We should continue to press our point firmly, but in a very temperate and unmenacing tone for the present. We can always stiffen up later, even on this particular question, if we think it desirable. That we are perfectly right on this question I cannot doubt. And it is not good business to give up altogether any really strong ground of complaint. But, in my opinion, it is hardly prudent *as yet* to treat the question in a manner which may compel us, in certain very conceivable contingencies, to choose between war and signal discredit. . . .

It was certainly not prudent. And his second intervention shows why. Had the Boers at that moment chosen to march there was nothing at all to stop them, all along the border of Natal and the Orange River frontier. Before there could be any question, as Milner saw it, of putting further pressure on the Transvaal Government on behalf of the Uitlanders, that situation had to be remedied. All appearance of building up an aggressive force had to be carefully avoided. On the other hand, Milner was convinced that an obviously defensive force would bring it home to the hotheads among the Boers that Great Britain was not as weak as she looked—as she has always and invariably looked when faced with trouble of any kind. And here already the disadvantages of the system made themselves apparent. Nothing could have been more reasonable than to spend a small sum right away on precautionary measures to save a much vaster sum and untold bloodshed later on. But it could not be done quietly. The Treasury and the country would want to know why, and all the publicity of a special supplementary vote for the War Office would cause any such move to be interpreted as a virtual declaration of war. Thus, while everybody agreed that something had to be done, it had to be done on the cheap:

When I left England [wrote Milner, again to Lord Selborne, from the liner taking him to Cape Town] the position of *the reinforcements question* was in a most unsatisfactory state. As usual, apparently, consideration of policy had to give way to economy, and Lansdowne told me, at an interview I had with him, Wolseley, and Buller at the W.O. . . . that it had been decided that any force sent should not cost more than £200,000. What utter futility it is to play with these huge risks in that style, I don't tell you, for, of course, you know it. But I take things as I find them. . . . What I beg you to do is to hang on like grim death to the decision to send reinforcements and not to let the Government slip out of it on any account. I am sure the Secretary of State [Joseph Chamberlain] is bent upon it, but you know the sort of way sometimes tacit opposition, the making of difficulties of detail, etc., gets round even strong resolutions on the part of a busy man, and there is no one in England who feels quite so strongly about this question of reinforcements as I do. . . . As to the absolute necessity of not playing these high games with no adequate force behind us, I shall never have but one opinion. I desire peace—honestly—and I hope to maintain it. But we cannot answer for the other side, and I shall never rest as long as we are in such a position that a sudden move on their part would involve us in discreditable disaster.

Thus, before he had even set foot in Africa and long before he joined issue with the Boers, the battle with Whitehall was on— a battle that in the upshot was to drag on drearily and exhaustingly until the very brink of disaster when Roberts and Kitchener were sent out to rescue the name of Britain—Roberts who had magnanimously offered his own services in the field, even while Milner was on the high seas, in case of war. 'I have a great regard and high respect for Sir Alfred Milner,' he wrote to Lord Lansdowne, 'and I am confident that I could work in harmony with him.'

When Milner said that nobody in England felt quite so strongly about the question of reinforcements as he, it was because he, more than anyone, envisaged the very real possibility of war. He gave his reasons, cool and clear, in the first letter to Lord Selborne from which we have already quoted:

> Where I differ from you is in thinking that our being compelled to have recourse to war is very improbable. If this were the only question [the Aliens Immigration Law] between us and the Transvaal and if it could be settled by itself and in cool blood, I should agree with you. It is next door to inconceivable that the Transvaal should prefer war to such a very moderate concession as that of discussing an Immigration Bill with us instead of forcing down our throats an Act concocted independently of us. But the question will not be dealt with apart, on its own merits, or in cool blood. The next six months are bound in any case to be a period of great irritation. The Boers are evidently in a highly nervous and excitable condition. The Rhodesites are, as far as I can judge, itching to involve us in a quarrel. The proceedings of the Committee [to enquire into the Jameson Raid] will tend to promote exasperation on both sides. Finally there is the indemnity [for damage caused by the Jameson Raid] to be settled, and a very nasty controversy will arise out of that. It is quite possible, in my judgment, that amid all these influences tending to discord, the Government of the S.A.R. may be tempted to take a definite

attitude about the question of the Aliens' Law, which they would
not take if the question stood alone.

These are not the words of the ordinary senior official, the
pure administrator, no matter how talented, on his way to a new
appointment. They are the words of a natural leader—or, more
accurately, of a man with the mind of a natural leader: the sort
of mind which is quite incapable of applying itself to any problem
without immediately stripping it down to its essentials and
deciding what should be done about it. In the Randolph Churchill
crisis the young private secretary to Lord Goschen saw in a flash
what his chief must do and threw his whole weight into seeing
that he did it. Now, and also in a flash, he has chosen his line in
South Africa—and even before writing to a boyhood friend,
almost certainly in all sincerity, to say that it was no good talking
about what he was going to do until he knew more about it—and,
hardly realising it, is already leading with all his might and
making policy for his masters with the instinctive and unconscious ease of the born statesman. From now on, as far as
Milner is concerned, the problem to decide is not how this extraordinary man succeeded as well as he did, but why he did not
rise to dominate his age. From now on, as far as South Africa
is concerned, everything follows naturally and with the in-
evitability of fate. Never has any man entrusted with a great and
delicate mission stared more straightly into the face of difficulty.
Never did any man stand in greater need of that clarity of gaze.

To begin with, the supreme problem of the moment, how to
check the Transvaal Government in its overweening behaviour
towards the British settlers without precipitating war, was merci-
fully easier than Milner had feared. The despatch about the Aliens
Act had been sent, backed not only by the reinforcements Milner
had demanded, but also by a naval demonstration off Delagoa
Bay. The Transvaal Government, with war and peace in the
balance, had climbed down and for some time adopted a more
conciliatory attitude. In May, Milner was able to cable to Joseph
Chamberlain, his chief at the Colonial Office: 'Effect of firm
attitude of H.M. Government has been to put rather more heart
into the Ministers and other timid people who begin to see that

firmness makes for peace, and strengthening garrison, instead of provoking Boers, has had effect of wholesome warning.'

The situation, broadly, was that the Cape Government, under Sir Gordon Sprigge, was afraid of the nationalist Afrikander Bond, led by Hofmeyer, and was under continual pressure from those Dutch politicians who could never make up their minds which side they were on until it was too late for them to throw their whole weight and prestige with their cousins in the Transvaal into the task of persuading Kruger and his hot-heads (outstanding among these was the youthful Smuts) to see reason. Milner referred to them again, but indirectly, in a private letter to Miss Synge: '. . . When I arrived here, everything looked desperately bad, and we were within an ace of a blow up. But the Boers thought better of it. They have not really changed. . . . But they have given way an inch and there is a respite. That, of course, so far, is good for me. But things all round are in a most rotten condition, and whether anything can be made of them for permanent good remains to be seen.'

At the same time he was worried lest, having made one effort and temporarily reduced the more blatant pretensions of the Transvaal Government, the British Government would sink back in the virtuous consciousness of a job well done and allow things to slide back into the bad old ways. This anxiety he expressed in a letter to the Governor of Natal, Sir W. Hely-Hutchinson: 'My only anxiety is lest people in England should think that we have gained more than we really have, and should consequently be too quick to relax that steady pressure on the Transvaal without which they will never do a thing.'

The more things change, the more they are the same. The whole question of what is nowadays known as appeasement, the habit of making concessions from weakness instead of expressing a conciliatory attitude from strength, in face of a determined and devious enemy, was plainly very much in Milner's mind from the moment of his appointment to the final catastrophe; and in August of that first year he seized on a question of Chamberlain's to elaborate his conviction in a letter which, had its contents been learned by heart and digested by modern statesmen before 1939, might have altered the course of recent history. Its message for us today is no less relevant; and its freshness, alas, seems likely to endure.

> There is one question to which I should like to reply at once, because it is of supreme importance, and I have no doubt whatever of the true answer. I refer to what you say about the Naval Demonstration and the increase of the garrison. The cost of the latter was, no doubt, considerable, but I am quite sure that the two measures between them averted war in South Africa. There are heavy clouds still on the horizon, but nothing like the imminent storm I found when I came here. Within a fortnight of my arrival the Government of the S.A.R. made a distinct retreat. It was due to one thing only, the impression made upon their minds by these two actions, which they regarded as a clear indication that we meant business, and they must yield or fight.

He went on to show, all importantly, that in his demand for an unambiguous display of resolution he was not in the least pursuing the policy of the big stick for its own sake. It was not a matter of frightening the Boers into total submission by an overwhelming show of force. Rather, it was a matter of indicating beyond all doubt that if they crossed a certain line it would mean war. The British Government had made up its mind about this: indeed, there was no escape from it. And Milner himself had nothing to do with this decision. What the British Government was failing to do was to make its decision quite clear to Kruger, who, inflated by the ease with which the British had allowed themselves to be pushed about in the past, might be expected to believe that he could repeat the performance of Majuba Hill.

Thus Milner continued:

> This is not my personal conviction merely. I have heard only one opinion on the subject from men who know South Africa and who could speak to me in confidence. My witnesses were all men who dreaded war. Some of them—notably one, a high Transvaal official —were sympathisers with the Boer cause. But they recognised that the danger was not that we should attack the Transvaal, but that the Transvaal would take up an attitude of defiance towards us which in self-defence we could not tolerate. People, who would not openly

say a word against the Transvaal, have implored me to impress upon the British Government that to take up and maintain a strong attitude and especially to keep such a force in our own country, as would impress the Boers with the *danger* of defying us, was the only way to avert the catastrophe which they dreaded. I am sure they are right. We have put our foot down and we must keep it there.

Finally, having said all that, having made his point that the only way to avoid war was for the British Government to persist in a genuine and unequivocal show of resolution, Milner went on to show that if the jingo extremists thought they had won a new and formidable recruit they deceived themselves. We must keep our foot down because, once having put it down, it would be fatal to relax, he said in effect. We have put it down because the Transvaal is pursuing certain policies which we cannot tolerate; and we must keep it down unless we want to tempt them into a position from which war is the only issue. This, as it were, is a matter of practical politics. But, he concluded, let us at least realise the difficulties of the other side and do all we can, by showing infinite patience, to help them to overcome their own difficulties and reach a point of stability from which they will be able to form a cooler judgement of South African realities: 'The internal state of the Transvaal is the danger to S. Africa. That country is in a terrible mess, social, political, and financial. I think great allowance must be made for the men who have to govern a country in that state, even if their methods often seem to us very unwise. We should be very patient with them, very conciliatory, remembering how much excuse they have for regarding us with suspicion. But we cannot afford to appear, or to be, weak. It is no use being conciliatory if people think you are only conciliatory because you are afraid. . . .'

That passage, with an alteration of two words, might stand and, indeed, should stand as a commentary on the conflict of half a century later, in which we are all engaged. More particularly, it once and for all disposes of the all-too-prevalent notion that Milner was a man of a rigid, inflexible, and doctrinaire cast of mind.

His task, as he saw it then—and he took it very quietly and

steadily, sorting out in his mind its many aspects—was above all
to exert a steady pressure on the Transvaal Government while
maintaining a genuinely conciliatory attitude. This involved
building up British strength in South Africa while restraining the
fire-eaters on his own side and avoiding all appearance of aggressive intent. At the same time he had to frustrate the manœuvres of
those among the Cape Dutch whom he knew to be disloyal,
while avoiding all speech and action which might antagonise
their colleagues, who, nevertheless, felt strong affinities with the
Boer cause. There were also the opportunists: a large number of
these, waiting to see which way the cat would jump before committing themselves, had to be impressed with the fact that the
British Government meant business. And more tiresome even
than these, because some of them held responsible posts in the
Administration, were the British fellow-travellers, who, from
sentiment or from a feeling that the future lay with the Boers,
could not be relied upon. Milner's own deputy High Commissioner and military commander-in-chief, General Butler,
was one of these, fantastic as it may seem.

As if all this was not enough, Milner had England to think
about too. There he had the great good fortune to be backed
steadfastly by his departmental chiefs, Chamberlain and Selborne.
But there were other departments involved, above all the War
Office (itself responsible for the selection of a pro-Boer to be
Milner's right-hand man); and there was the perpetual threat
from politicians, interested in party advantage more than in the
future of their country, to make hay with his dispositions—to
say nothing of the sentimental-humanitarian opposition, which
saw the Boers as a simple race of pastoral philosophers. England
too, and indeed all Europe, was vulnerable to the propaganda of
peripatetic Boers who were sent abroad by Kruger to employ
their native 'slimness' in seducing Whitehall into weakening its
purposes, to supply the Opposition, to say nothing of hostile
powers in Europe, with ammunition against the Government's
policy, and to arrange for a continuous supply of arms. Chief
among these was the Johannesburg lawyer-politician, Leyds,
who, with Smuts at Kruger's elbow, formed part of the small

group of fanatical advocates of a final show-down with the might of Britain.

If it is argued that it is absurd to praise a man for a policy that failed, the answer here is that Milner's policy was in fact never tried. In spite of the efforts of the Colonial Office to give him their full support, his policy of conciliation from what would nowadays be called a position of strength was hamstrung in a thousand different ways. When the Boers invaded Natal they had 90,000 men, about half of them in the field, and all trained to the country. They had 110 guns and a vast store of rifles and ammunition, much of which had reached them via the British territory of the Cape, thanks to the connivance of the supposedly loyal government of Cape Colony. Opposed to them were 27,000 British, including 11,000 in Cape Colony, half of them locally raised forces. This general situation, if not the war itself, was due largely to the British military machine, which was seen functioning at its preposterous norm in the appointment of Butler as a political general, and, later, Buller, as Commander-in-Chief. Twenty years earlier, after the brilliant success of Roberts at Kandahar, Lord Salisbury had murmured: 'Would that the Queen were as well served in Africa as in Asia!' Milner might well have echoed him, and all the more since Roberts himself had already volunteered to go out to South Africa with Milner and serve under him. Instead, in October 1898 when the crisis was fast growing, the War Office chose Lieut.-General Sir William Butler.

This was an episode which not only throws additional light on Milner's character, but also, in its deadly serious slapstick, exposes better than anything else the forgotten little fact that his policy never had a chance. Butler was appointed without consultation with either the Colonial Office or the High Commissioner. He was an Irishman, brilliant and charming. He was also, as was generally known, an ardent sympathiser with any anti-British cause he could find. Already earlier in South Africa, and again in Egypt, he had been at the centre of anti-British intrigues, while officially representing the Queen. His conduct was invariably from the best of motives; for he too, in his way, may be said to have been born before his time. He believed that all wars were deliberately fomented for their own nefarious ends by big business and high finance. The only thing that is not clear is why, believing this, he went on being a soldier. Both in his telegrams to Chamberlain, while Milner was at home on a short visit, and in his own autobiography he was disarmingly explicit about his attitude to the Transvaal troubles. All the grievances of the Uitlanders, he said, were a put-up job, part of a calculated ramp of 'a colossal syndicate for the spread of misrepresentation', a syndicate organised by the Randlords, who were concerned only with the rape of gold and precious stones for transhipment 'to another hemisphere for the profit of the alien'.

That sort of view was well enough in a Campbell-Bannerman; it would have passed in a regimental soldier; but it was not the sort of view to be tolerated in the man chosen to uphold Great Britain's interests in South Africa. It was, however, tolerated. The Colonial Office had to knuckle under to Sir Garnet Wolseley at the War Office. Milner at first took no notice. To a letter wryly describing to Sir Walter Hely-Hutchinson the sort of mess he found things in when he returned from his London visit, he appended one of his postscripts: 'Don't think Butler is a bad fellow. He is hasty and rhetorical, fearfully deficient in judgement. But he is well-meaning enough and a most agreeable companion.'

But as the crisis developed, the impossibility of the situation became increasingly evident, and in June 1899 Milner had to admit to himself that the General, far from contenting himself with holding (and expressing) views diametrically opposed to his own and the British Government's, was actively hindering the proper execution of official policy. He was refusing, that is to say, to make the necessary defensive dispositions and persuading the War Office, which needed very little persuasion, that there was no need for the reinforcements his chief was demanding. It was only at this point that Milner at last demanded his recall. But he was made to endure for two more months. To recall General Butler in the middle of a crisis, Chamberlain replied, would be interpreted by the Boers as an unfriendly act.

As for Milner's forebodings about the reliability of the Cape Government, it was not until after the war that the justice of these was brought home—and then it was too late. A glimpse of the 'rottenness' to which Milner briefly referred in his letter to Miss Synge is found in the correspondence that went on between the Afrikander promoters of the final conference between Kruger and Milner. Thus we find Mr. J. X. Merriman, Treasurer-General of the pro-Boer government of Cape Colony, writing to President Steyn of the Orange Free State:

> I had the other day . . . several talks with Lippert about the Transvaal. He takes a very sane view of matters there, and is very hopeless. He represents Kruger—as others describe him—as more dogged and bigoted than ever, and surrounded by a crew of self-seekers who prevent him from seeing straight. He has no one to whom he turns for advice, and is so inflated as to have the crazy belief that he (Kruger) is born to bring about peace between Germany and France! If he falls, or dies, who have we to look to? All this plays the game of Rhodes and his brother capitalists. Is there no opportunity of bringing about a *rapprochement* between us, in which the Free State might play the part of honest broker? . . .

And again:

> One cannot conceal the fact that the greatest danger to the future lies in the attitude of President Kruger and his vain hope of building up a State on a foundation of a narrow unenlightened minority, and his obstinate rejection of all prospect of using the materials which lie ready to his hand to establish a true Republic on a broad liberal basis. The report of recent discussions in the Volksraad on his finances and their mismanagement fill one with apprehension. Such a state of affairs cannot last, it must break down from inherent rottenness, and it will be well if the fall does not sweep away the freedom of all of us. . . .

These indictments of the Transvaal Government were written not by Milner but, privately, by one of the men who in public dared not say a word against Kruger, and who failed utterly to rise to the occasion by lending their weight publicly to influence the Transvaal with advice which had it come from an Englishman would have been instantly rejected. It is worth noting in this context that the British seem to have been the only people in the world who were unaware of the true state of affairs in the Transvaal, in spite of Milner's desperate attempts to bring the matter home. In 1898 when Dr. Leyds toured Europe, amongst other things in an attempt to raise a loan, each European government to whom he applied, including those who were only too pleased to use the South African trouble as a stick to beat England with, refused absolutely unless the Transvaal would guarantee to reform itself from top to bottom.

Chapter Nine

GRAAF REINET

T WAS AGAINST this sort of background that Milner made
his first great speech in Africa, which was also, perhaps, the
greatest of his career. For over a year he had waited without
committing himself, in the hope that the Transvaal Government
might choose to see the light. This was the origin of the legend
that Milner was slow to make up his mind; but in fact, as we have
seen, his mind was made up from the beginning, and he waited
only in the hope that events might cause him to change it. Events
did not; and the re-election of Kruger by an overwhelming
majority in February of 1898 made it clear that they never would.
For a year he had seen the Transvaal Dutch presuming on his
forbearance by postponing necessary reforms and rejecting with
increasing contumely his private and far from tactless suggestions
(for it should be made clear that Milner did not resort to blunt-
ness until he had exhausted all the arts of persuasion: he was invariably at pains to combine his private warnings with public
discretion). Now Kruger's first act on his return to power was to
attack the independence of the judiciary by dismissing the Chief
Justice, Sir John G. Kotze. In a situation which foreshadowed
what was to happen in Cape Town fifty years later, Kruger had
challenged the power of the judges to test all laws passed by the
Volksraad by reference to the Constitution. Kotze's dismissal
was the inevitable outcome of the President's decision to destroy
the independence of the courts and subordinate them to the
Volksraad. It was also a public and final demonstration of the truth
of all that Milner had come to believe about the internal state of
the Transvaal. The Cape Dutch, however, still raised no word
against Kruger, and the High Commissioner decided that the time
had come to clarify his own position in public, and at the same

time to tell the Cape Dutch that he would like them to make up their minds as to whose side they were on. At best they were then sitting on the fence; at worst they were intriguing with the Transvaal Boers against the British, towards whom they professed their loyalty, and under whose protection they lived and flourished.

'There has got to be a separation of the sheep from the goats', Milner wrote to Sir Walter Hely-Hutchinson, with whom he corresponded constantly on the history then being made; 'a separation', in the words of Mr. Headlam, 'of those who disapproved of the dishonest despotism at Pretoria, from those who admired and truckled to it.'

Milner was on tour, and the address of loyalty presented to him at Graaf Reinet in March 1898, gave him the occasion he required. He seized it in one of the most striking utterances ever made in a moment of crisis. The local Afrikander Bond in their address of welcome took occasion to protest the loyalty of the Bond, while complaining that in certain quarters that loyalty had been impugned. They therefore requested the High Commissioner to clear them from such slanders in the eyes of the Queen. After replying to the address in conventional terms, that same night Milner went over to the attack. He had found what he had been seeking, an opportunity to put the ambiguities of the Cape Dutch quite publicly in the light in which for long he had seen them privately:

> I should have been glad to avoid any reference to political questions tonight [he told his unsuspecting audience], but I have been put into a position in which it is impossible for me entirely to ignore them. I cannot, without discourtesy, disregard altogether the terms of the address which was presented to me today by the local members of the Afrikander Bond. That address protested in somewhat vehement terms against the charges of disloyalty, which it alleged had been directed against the Bond, and it suggested that I should take steps to clear the character of that organisation.

He then proceeded to put those responsible firmly in their place:

> Really, gentlemen, I think the request a little unreasonable. We

are just entering upon a season of electioneering. If, in addition to discharging my own ordinary business (which pretty well fills my day), I had to correct all the unfair and exaggerated statements which at election times are made by every party against every other party, I should not only have to work all day, but to sit up all night. I really think I am much better in bed. . . .

After that unequivocal opening he took up the subject of loyalty:

> Of course I am glad to be assured that any section of Her Majesty's subjects are loyal, but I should be much more glad to be allowed to take that for granted. Why should I not? What reason could there be for disloyalty? You have thriven wonderfully well under Her Majesty's rule.

And so he moved into a detailed exposition of the benefits of British rule in the Cape, benefits known well to all his audience, and, when listed, made all the more telling by the unspoken comparison, vivid in the minds of them all, between British tolerance and the despotism of the Transvaal:

> . . . You live under an absolutely free system of government [he concluded, passing from the material to the spiritual benefits], protecting the rights, and encouraging the spirit of independence, of every citizen. You have courts of law, manned by men of the highest ability and integrity, and secure in the discharge of their high functions from all danger of external interference. You have, at least as regards the white races, perfect equality of citizenship. And these things have not been won from a reluctant sovereign. They have been gladly and freely bestowed upon you, because freedom and self-government, justice and equality are the first principles of British policy. And they are secured to you by the strength of the power that gave them, whose navy protects your shores from attack, without your being asked to contribute one pound to that protection, unless you yourselves desire it. Well, gentlemen, of course you are loyal. It would be monstrous if you were not.

But that was far from the end. There was a reason for this sensitiveness to charges of disloyalty, and Milner was going to expose it. Of course, he argued, the bulk of the population were perfectly loyal where all domestic questions were concerned. But more than domestic questions were concerned.

What gives the sting to the charge of disloyalty in this case, what makes it stick, and what makes people wince under it, is the fact that the political controversies of this country at present unfortunately turn largely upon another question—I mean the relations of Her Majesty's Government to the South African Republic—and that, whenever there is any prospect of a difference between these two parties, a number of people in the colony at once vehemently, and without even the semblance of impartiality, espouse the side of the Republic.

He did not think this meant they were disloyal. 'I am familiar at home with the figure of the politician—often the best of men, though singularly injudicious—who, whenever any dispute arises with another country, starts with the assumption that his own country must be wrong.' But if they were not disloyal, they must not be surprised at seeming so, at least those who 'seem to care much more for the independence of the Transvaal than they do for the honour and the interests of the country to which they themselves belong'.

But there was still another point he wanted to make, and a most important point at that. If, as he believed, the main object of the supporters of the Transvaal cause was to make Britain think twice about her policy to the Transvaal, they were as wrong as could be, and he proceeded to explain precisely why:

For this policy of theirs rests on the assumption that Great Britain has some occult design on the independence of the Transvaal—an independence which she herself has given—and that she is seeking causes of quarrel, in order to take this independence away. But that assumption is the exact opposite of the truth. So far from seeking causes of quarrel, the constant desire of the British Government is to avoid causes of quarrel, and not to take up lightly the complaints (and they are numerous) which reach it from British subjects within the Transvaal; for the very reason that it wishes to avoid even the semblance of interference in the internal affairs of that country, while, as regards external affairs, it insists only on that minimum of control which it has always distinctly reserved, and has reserved, I may add, solely in the interests of the future tranquillity of South Africa. That is Great Britain's moderate attitude, and she cannot be frightened out of it.

And then, finally, after telling the Bond with the utmost candour what he thought of them, after emphasising the futility of their behaviour, and after putting the responsibility for discord firmly on the shoulders of the Transvaal Government, he suddenly held out his hand, and, as it were, taking his audience into his confidence, went on to finish on a note of genuine conciliation:

> Now, I wish to be perfectly fair. Therefore let me say that this suspicion, though absolutely groundless, is not, after all that has happened, altogether unnatural. I accept the situation that at the present moment any advice that I could tender, or that any of your British fellow-citizens could tender, to the Government of the Transvaal, though it might be the best advice in the world, would instantly be rejected, because it was British. But the same does not apply to the Dutch citizens of this Colony, and especially to those who have gone so far in the expression of their sympathy for the Transvaal, as to expose themselves to those charges of disloyalty to their own flag. Their good will at least cannot be suspected across the border ... then let them use all their influence, which is bound to be great, not in encouraging the Government of the Transvaal in obstinate resistance to all reform, but in inducing it gradually to assimilate its institutions, and what is even more important than institutions, the temper and spirit of its administration, to those of the free communities of South Africa, such as this colony or the Orange Free State. That is the direction in which a peaceful way out of these inveterate troubles, which have now plagued this country for more than thirty years, is to be found. ...

The effect of this performance was electrifying. It sounded the clearest note of warning that had yet been heard. It stated unequivocally the position of the High Commissioner, who until then had striven his utmost to keep out of and above the party quarrel. It told all concerned, once and for all, who were Milner's friends and who his enemies. And it rallied as nothing else could have done the true loyalists among both British and Dutch, not only in the Cape, but in every part of South Africa. Some idea of the effect of the Graaf Reinet speech on the Uitlanders in the Transvaal may be gained from a farewell letter to Milner, written six years later, by Sir Percy Fitzpatrick, who, in the hour of

Milner's departure, flew back in memory to the Graaf Reinet occasion as to an act of liberation: '... *You* don't know the feeling of gratitude and relief that we felt—almost bewildering relief— when the Graaf Reinet speech removed the load of doubt and per- plexity, and gave to the faith that was in our blood and our bones the chance to rise again and bear fruit. . . . It made a world of difference to be able to believe again, and feel that at last we had to deal with one who saw clearly and would hold fast. . . .'

Chapter Ten

'THE CASE FOR INTERVENTION'

THE GRAAF REINET speech sounded the note of Milner's whole administration for all to hear. It still gives the measure of his wisdom as a statesman and his skill as a politician. It was praised for 'its wisdom, courage, and yet conciliatory spirit' by the British Press, including the Liberal *Daily News*; and, in fact, everybody, except those who were firmly convinced that the whole case against the Transvaal Government was based on a capitalist plot hatched by the mining syndicates, had to admit the sober brilliance of Milner's counter-attack. Although in his own mind he had for some time been convinced of the impossibility of coming to an accommodation with the Transvaal Boers, he had never yet publicly spoken on the situation in all its gravity. Now, in that one speech, he revealed all at once his attitude, his determination, his character, and his formidable skill. It is difficult to know whether most to admire the courage of his outspokenness, the straightness of his eye, the extraordinary way in which he combined didactic candour and positive castigation with a disarmingly conciliatory air, or the subtlety with which he contrived to manœuvre the burghers of Graaf Reinet, and with them the whole Afrikander population of Cape Colony, into accepting service in his cause or putting themselves in the wrong.

In a word, this speech makes nonsense of the idea that Milner was deficient in diplomatic flexibility and subtlety; within the necessary framework of his entrenched position, he was as subtle as the serpent. He also believed in honesty, and it is worth noting that his contempt for that exercise of stupid and crude dishonesty characteristically known to its exponents as finessing was not directed only at his enemies. In September of the same year, when the pro-British 'Progressive' party had, by the narrowest of margins, been defeated at the poll by the Afrikander Bond, its leaders, Sprigg and Rhodes, had a scheme to turn the tables. Milner, as Governor, refused absolutely to countenance their elaborate and wanton exercise in gerrymandering; and this in spite of the fact that he passionately wanted to see the Progressives in power, as the only means to what might have been the last hope of South Africa, a federation of the British colonies.

Though, of course, I want Sprigg to stay in [he wrote to Lord Selborne], I disbelieve absolutely in the policy of such tactics. But that is not my business. The question is, whether I am personally to facilitate their being adopted by assisting to put off the meeting of the House. I will do no such thing. R.H., C.J.R., J.G.S., and Co., steadily refuse to see that there is a moral side to such matters or even that *straightforwardness* may have a tactical value. . . . Anyway, I am quite determined not to put myself into a position in which, if the edifice does collapse, my own credit, and that of the Imperial Govt. and of the British system in this Colony will fall with it. . . .

And in a postscript he added:

Curious psychologically how the present Rhodes cum Harris scheme for keeping office *per fas et nefas* is just the Raid over again. I mean it is the same attempt to gain prematurely by violent and unscrupulous means what you could get honestly and without violence, if you would only *wait and work for it*. I am sick of hearing that if the loyal Ministry lose office for a single day, the party will go to pieces, Rhodes and Compy will throw up the game in disgust and the Imperial cause in S. Africa will be ruined. Captain of XI to umpire: 'Unless you cheat, I won't play.' What rubbish!

Milner too, nevertheless, had been driven to the conclusion that the time for patience was coming to an end for some time before these strictures on the policies of Rhodes, whom he otherwise profoundly admired. The Graaf Reinet speech was the first public indication that he was preparing to take the initiative; but behind that speech there lay a conviction deeper than it was either desirable or proper to express that no good could come of forbearance. On the day after the dismissal of the Chief Justice of the Transvaal he was finally convinced, and almost at once he sent off to Chamberlain an official despatch, and, after it, a long explanatory letter. The letter shows clearly the state of mind behind the Graaf Reinet speech and gives a complete outline of the general situation as it appeared to Milner in March of 1898.

The long despatch which goes to you by this mail about our differences with the Transvaal, is written with a purpose. I am afraid that after a few months' respite, we are once more on the verge of serious trouble with the Boers; the despatch is one which, if things get worse, it may be useful some day to publish. But, of course, *only if things get worse*. My reason in writing this letter is to warn you privately, that I think there is a very great probability that they will. There is no way out of the political troubles of S. Africa except reform in the Transvaal or war. And at present the chances of reform in the Transvaal are worse than ever. The Boers quarrel bitterly among themselves, but it is about jobs and contracts, not politics! In their determination to keep all power in their own hands and to use it with a total disregard of the interests of the unenfranchised, as well as in their own hatred and suspicion of Great Britain, the vast majority of them are firmly united.

He went on to give a swift recension of the course of events since his arrival in South Africa.

For a few months after I came here things began to look a little better. I began to hope that we might get, not indeed on to good, but on to tolerable terms with them, that though the fundamental antagonism might remain unaltered, a few minor concessions on their part, a few small courtesies on ours, might serve to conceal it, to allow us to attend to our own business, and them to muddle on in their own way, and ultimately to develop political parties amongst themselves, which would compete for the support of the Uitlander. These hopes have so far been disappointed, and since the beginning of the autumn . . . any little signs of consideration for the subject races of the Transvaal, whether European or native, and of civility to us, have ceased to appear. . . . Kruger has returned to power, more autocratic and more reactionary than ever. . . . He has immense resources in money and any amount of ammunitions of war, to which he is constantly adding. Politically he has strengthened his hold on the Orange Free State, and the Colonial Afrikanders continue to do obeisance before him. And not only the Afrikanders. . . . Under the circumstances, I conceive that it depends entirely on Leyds' estimate of the general European situation, whether we do or do not get an embarrassingly rude answer to the despatch on the

Suzerainty question. Of one thing I am certain. Kruger will never take any step which he thinks will provoke us to fight. But if he is assured that our hands are full in other directions he will certainly seize the opportunity to assert his independence in a very pointed way. That is one danger, but it is not the only one. There are several questions at issue between ourselves and the Boers, on which we are pressing them for redress. There are others hanging over our heads, on which it will be extremely difficult for us to refrain from doing the same. I am quite sure we shall only get evasive answers, or no answers at all. We may even get more or less insolent ones, though, as a complete disregard of our remonstrances does just as well, I don't know why they should be at pains to be actively rude. And while they have many opportunities of annoying or slighting us, we have practically no means of annoying or frightening them except those adopted—with success—last spring, but which from the nature of the case cannot be frequently repeated. The demonstration of last spring was effective, because it was exceptional. But if recurrent demonstrations of that kind were to become a regular incident of our dealings with the Transvaal, they would presently come to be as little regarded as our written protests already are. I dislike multiplying these written protests and, however disagreeable it may be to be treated as non-existent, I think I had better not add to the number, unless I have reason to think that, in spite of all the troubles we have on our hands in other directions, we should be justified in bringing our long controversy to a head. *Looking at the question from a purely S. African point of view,* I should be inclined to work up to a crisis, not indeed by looking about for causes of complaint or making a fuss about trifles, but by steadily and inflexibly pressing for the redress of substantial wrongs and injustices. It would not be difficult thus to work up an extremely strong *cumulative case.* . . . . What, in my judgment, is inexpedient in such critical relations between us and the Transvaal, is to deal with single questions singly. Our action on any one must depend on our attitude to all. . . .

It is not difficult to imagine the consternation in Whitehall caused by the very idea of deliberately working things up to a crisis, in the full knowledge that it might lead straight to war. It says a great deal for both Chamberlain and Selborne that although both were deeply perturbed by this flagrant contravention of the

whole British instinct for *laisser aller* and muddling through, they
did not panic, even when, a week later, Milner presented them,
in a nasty development of the case of the Chief Justice, with
what he took to be a cast-iron case for the strongest British
intervention. Instead they answered him with extreme reasonableness, stating that 'the principal object of H.M. Government in
S. Africa at present is peace. Nothing but a most flagrant offence
would justify the use of force', and going on, first Chamberlain,
then Selborne, to put the case against bringing things to a head,
and setting out the political conditions, both at home and in
South Africa, which it would be necessary to secure before war
could be seriously contemplated. The correspondence continued
into the summer, and it looked for a time as though the worst
might happen, characterised by Selborne as 'simply a first-class
calamity', namely the development of a serious difference of
opinion between Milner and his chiefs. But in fact there was no
difference of opinion, as such. There was simply a difference of
approach, not merely to the Transvaal, but to all political questions, now dramatised in the Transvaal controversy. Fundamentally, it was the difference between Milner and what one might
call the British school of politics, which was to drive him into
retirement for thirteen years, and upon which we shall have to
dwell soon. The particular focus of cross-purposes was Chamberlain's attitude to what would make a *casus belli*. Chamberlain
insisted that only a serious and flagrant breach of the Convention
would suffice. Milner's attitude was that to lay so much stress on
the technicalities of the Convention was disastrous and misleading.

> I should say the time had come to make it clear [he wrote to Lord
> Selborne] that—quite apart from Conventions—there was a degree
> of lawless tyranny, as well as of offensiveness towards ourselves,
> which we were not prepared to put up with in a neighbouring State,
> in which our interests are so great and the condition of which reacts
> so powerfully on our own possessions. . . . What I am driving at is
> our concern with the Transvaal apart from all Conventions, which
> is far more important than our rights under these miserable docu-
> ments. . . . I agree with you that an open denunciation of either of the

existing Conventions is most improbable. I have never feared—or hoped—for it. What object could the S.A.R. have in denouncing a Convention, when it is so easy to interpret it away and then tell us, if we don't like the interpretation, to call in an arbitrator? But my point is that, even if they observed the Conventions, and that in their obvious intention and not merely in the minimising sense which they seek to put upon them, we should still not be out of the wood. I think there is a positive danger of the C.O. losing sight of the essentials of S. African policy over the technicalities of these wretched Treaties. . . . We seem to regard them, not only as giving us certain rights—mostly worthless—but as precluding us from that interest and—in the last resort—interference in the internal affairs of the Transvaal which by the nature of things every state has in the internal affairs of its neighbours, when they directly and vitally affect its own internal affairs. That is the position of British South Africa.

Milner also believed that time was not on the side of England, and that Kruger's building up of a strong and well-equipped army with money obtained from taxing the Uitlanders, added incalculably to the cost of every delay in a final settlement. But he reconciled himself to his instructions and settled down loyally to play a waiting game. 'We must keep up our wickets but not attempt to force the game', he telegraphed one of his subordinates. They did so, and for another year affairs dragged on, with incident after incident, handled with total forbearance on Milner's part, until the crisis of the Uitlander's petition in March 1899.

The condition of Your Majesty's subjects in this State has indeed become wellnigh intolerable. The acknowledged and admitted grievances, of which Your Majesty's subjects complained, prior to 1895, not only are not redressed, but exist today in an aggravated form. They are still deprived of all political rights, they are denied any voice in the Government of the country, they are taxed far above the requirements of the country, the revenue of which is misapplied and devoted to objects which keep alive a continuous and well-founded feeling of irritation, without in any way advancing the general interest of the State. Maladministration and peculation of public moneys go hand in hand, without any vigorous measures being adopted to put a stop to the scandal. The education of the Uitlander children is made subject to impossible conditions. The police afford no adequate protection to the lives and properties of the inhabitants of Johannesburg; they are rather a source of danger to the peace and safety of the Uitlander population.

Even then, and when Chamberlain asked Milner to prepare a special despatch elaborating his views in terms which could, unlike his secret despatches, be published, his loyalty to the Colonial Office and his extreme anxiety in no way to embarrass Chamberlain led him to understate his case, as he saw it. In a private covering letter to Lord Selborne, dated April 5th, we find him saying: 'My own view is in my secret despatches—only not quite so strongly put as what I really feel. I don't want to give you the impression that *I wish to rush you*. And I am painfully conscious that what is to us all here an all-overshadowing nightmare, precluding any other work of a more useful kind, is to people at home a matter of faint interest exciting only a very small degree of public attention. It is odd that it should be so, seeing the enormous material value of the thing involved, as well as the plainness of the moral issue. But so it apparently is.'

The celebrated despatch itself, called by Mr. L. S. Amery 'one of the most masterly State documents ever penned', was dated the previous day, April 14th, 1899. In it he withheld nothing of himself, and he committed himself, no longer tentatively and in private to his Chief and colleagues, but for all the world to see and judge, to the case for intervention. More than once in his life, in private letters to friends, he had taken comfort in the thought that, in the last resort, he did not care what happened to him—he was unmarried, he had no ties, he was uninterested in a career as such. This despatch, in which he offered himself up without concealment, vulnerable to the blind brutality of public criticism, the unscrupulous contrivers of party capital, and the risk of being disowned by his own masters, was the first great act which gave positive proof that this attitude was true and that his disdain for personal advancement and public reputation was genuine and absolute. It was by no means the last. But here, more than at any other moment in his career, was the decisive action which, one way or another, could only make him or break him. It made him. A good deal was to happen in the next six months before war was finally declared, but nothing to change the fundamental situation here exposed.

In it Milner summed up the situation as he saw it, as he had already exposed it many times before, but this time stripping it bare to the one essential issue: 'the political turmoil in the Transvaal Republic will never end till the permanent Uitlander population is admitted to a share in the Government'. This was to be his touchstone in the negotiations that followed. It was to secure this end that he was ready to go to war. It was an end directed not at incorporating the Transvaal into the British Empire, but at achieving, through the influence of non-Dutch settlers, above all the British, a reformed and stable government in the Transvaal which would put an end to the dangerous tensions existing in South Africa, to say nothing of the Boer dream of driving the British out of Cape Colony. 'While that turmoil lasts there will be no tranquillity or adequate progress in Her Majesty's South African Dominions.'

After describing the position of those foreign settlers, mostly British, who were condemned to live without a voice in the government and in 'permanent subjection to the ruling caste which owes its wealth and power to their exertion', he went on to reveal his ultimate purpose, which very definitely did not include the subjugation of the Boers by British might:

The relations between the British Colonists and the two Republics are intimate to a degree which one must live in South Africa in order fully to realise. Socially, economically, ethnologically, they are all one country, the two white races are everywhere inextricably mixed up: it is absurd for either to dream of subjugating the other. The only condition in which they can live in harmony and the country progress is equality all round. South Africa can prosper under two, three, or six Governments, though the fewer the better, but not under two absolutely conflicting social and political systems, perfect equality for Dutch and British in the British Colonies side by side with permanent subjection of British to Dutch in one of the Republics. It is idle to talk of peace and unity under such a state of affairs.

It is this which makes the internal condition of Transvaal Republic a matter of vital interest to Her Majesty's Government. . . .

And again:

The true remedy is to strike at the root of all these injuries, the political impotence of the injured. What diplomatic protests will never accomplish, a fair measure of Uitlander representation would gradually but surely bring about. It seems a paradox but it is true that the only effective way of protecting our subjects is to help them to cease to be our subjects. The admission of Uitlanders to a fair share of political power would no doubt give stability to the Republic. But it would at the same time remove most of our causes of difference with it, and modify and in the long run entirely remove that intense suspicion and bitter hostility to Great Britain which at present dominates its internal and external policy.

And finally, in a plea for decisive action, a positive demand, backed by an unmistakable show of intention, for Uitlander enfranchisement, he commits himself for good or ill:

The case for intervention is overwhelming. The only attempted answer is that things will right themselves if left alone. But, in fact, the policy of leaving things alone has been tried for years, and it has led to their going from bad to worse.

Chapter Eleven

ULTIMATUM AND WAR

ON THAT DESPATCH Milner rested, and it was only a question of whether the Home Government would act on the Petition or not. It decided to act. But before Chamberlain's despatch was ready or Milner's published (it was a month before this was done, and even then the most revealing references to the war preparations of the Transvaal Government were omitted) the Cape Colony Government and the Government of the Orange Free State made a belated and last-minute effort to retrieve a situation which, with a little more honesty of purpose, they could have prevented from developing. They developed a plan, which fitted in with the decision of Milner and the Colonial Office, to arrange a conference between President Kruger and the High Commissioner. In it may be seen the forerunner of those conferences between heads of states, possessed by irreconcilable ambitions or ideas, which were to become a feature of the political landscape a few decades later—conferences which can end only in one of two ways: in stalemate or in surrender by one side. The Bloemfontein Conference ended in stalemate.

It took place against an unpleasant background of duplicity, the men who arranged it still finding themselves unable to speak of the Transvaal Government publicly in the terms of total disparagement which they habitually used in private. We have already seen the sort of correspondence which had been going on between the Dutch Ministers of the Cape Colony Government, who owed their loyalty to the Crown, and their opposite numbers in the Orange Free State, who did not. On the very eve of the Conference we find Mr. Merriman writing to Mr. Fischer:

> It will be a deplorable thing after all the trouble you have taken to bring about a meeting between the High Commissioner and the

President if nothing comes of it. .... I am sure that you will, and I most strongly urge you to use your utmost influence to bear on President Kruger to concede some colourable measure of reform, not so much in the interests of outsiders as in those of his own State. Granted that he does nothing. What is the future? His Boers, the backbone of the country, are perishing off the land; hundreds have become impoverished loafers, landless hangers-on of the town population. In his own interests he should recruit his Republic with new blood—and the sands are running out. I say this irrespective of agitation about Uitlanders. The fabric will go to pieces of its own accord unless something is done. ....

This was the picture of Kruger's republic as seen not by Milner or anybody at Government House, but by a well-wisher who preferred not to say publicly what he privately thought. It is not the picture of a prosperous, agrarian, God-fearing band of brothers being threatened by the industrial might of an aggressive foreign power.

Nothing was done. The President of the South African Republic and the British High Commissioner met as apparitions from two different worlds. In Mr. Headlam's words:

The stage was set and the play began. No drama could be more intense than the duel which ensued between these two strong, determined men. On the one side sat the cultured Englishman, single-handed, wise and iron-willed, fully aware that failure must mean ignominy or war; inexorably resolved to establish the rights of British citizens settling overseas and the position of Great Britain as the Paramount Power in South Africa. On the other side was the burly Voortrekker in his tightly-buttoned frock-coat; a cunning and equally strong-willed Dutchman, rooted in the ambition of a lifetime to establish his country as the predominant State in an all-Dutch Republic; who had fought England before, and won; who at his last meeting with a British High Commissioner had triumphantly hectored and tricked Sir Hercules Robinson after the Jameson Raid; who believed that God and the Liberal party would always be on his side in his determination to prevent foreigners from having a voice in the government of his country. Nor was he alone in that obstinate refusal. The temper of his burghers was at least as recalcitrant as his own. The recent election had shown that not only the old burghers, but also the younger leaders of the Afrikander party were as fanatical and ambitious as the President himself. 'Even if he promises concessions', a member of the Raad stated at this time, 'we who represent the people will not confirm them and Paul Kruger knows it. . . . He is losing his influence by his concessions. . . . It is the unanimous feeling in the Raad that there will be war. . . . We are ready for it!'

There were no adequate concessions from the man 'who had fought England before, and won'. The whole conference was dyed deep in the profound but, alas, all too natural illusion that the England which had thrown up the sponge after Majuba Hill was not in deadly earnest now. There were indeed pretended concessions. Kruger was ready to talk about everything but the enfranchisement, on clear but extremely moderate terms, of the Uitlanders. Milner would talk of nothing else. This was the central issue, and to this he stuck, disconcerting even the most obstinate member of an obstinate race by his tenacity. But Kruger would not concede.

For, to his mind, concession of the franchise meant only one thing, the inevitable subjection of the Government to the voting power of the majority of the inhabitants. Of himself and all that he stood for, the monopolies and concessions, the control of the Judiciary, the corrupt police, the harsh treatment of the natives, and the hope of establishing the supremacy of Dutch Afrikanderdom throughout South Africa, that in time must prove the end. This was the meaning of his outburst, as the Conference drew to a close. 'It is our country that you want', the old man cried, as he bent his head between his hands, and tears coursed down his rugged cheeks. In a sense he was right, but not in the sense he meant. There was no desire to wrest from the Boers the hard-won independence to which they clung so tenaciously. But the clash of two civilisations was ringing within those four walls, as the old President and the virile High Commissioner sat and wrestled in words. Conflict and tragedy were indeed inherent in the scene, created by the waves of the incoming tide of industrial self-governing civilisation, ever beating more strongly against the rigid barrier of a primitive, pastoral and oligarchic community, recently corrupted by the sudden acquisition of great wealth.

What followed belongs to the story of the Boer War rather

than to the story of Milner. Matters were now out of his hands, although there were four months still to go before the war started, months of the utmost personal strain for him, as the Home Government on the one hand strove with all its might to avert the impending conflict, looking for every possible loophole, and time and again seizing on Kruger's inadequate concessions and misleading offers to postpone the inevitable, while on the other it devoted itself to the task of bringing round public opinion to the view that this time the Transvaal must be settled once for all, even if it had to be done by war. Milner, though in his heart he now believed war to be unavoidable, and though under the most constant and harassing pressure from the loyalists in South Africa, who had already reached the same conclusion, supported his Government most steadfastly; and it speaks volumes for his own strength of character and for the patience and imagination of Chamberlain and Lord Selborne that during this waiting period when nerves and tempers were strained to the utmost, no serious rift came between them.

The idea of war with the S.A.R. is very distasteful to most people [wrote Lord Selborne on June 25th]. Consequently the Cabinet have undoubtedly had to modify the pace that they contemplated moving at immediately after the Bloemfontein Conference. There is no idea of receding from the intervention which was commenced by your action at Bloemfontein and our reply to the petition, but we simply cannot force the pace. We have between us moved public opinion, almost universally, forward to the position of accepting the eventual responsibility of seeing a remedy applied, and this is a great step forward; but we have not convinced them yet either that you can't believe a word Kruger says, or that he never has yielded and never will yield until he feels the muzzle of the pistol on his forehead, or that the surest way to avoid war is to prepare openly for war. . . . We have entered a lane, you have entered a lane, the Cabinet has entered a lane, the country has entered a lane, where no turning back is possible without humiliation and disaster. We must eventually force the door at the other end, by peaceful pressure if possible, but if necessary by war.

The Cabinet did its utmost to behave as though the threat of war did not exist. It encouraged the mediation of the Bond leader, Mr. Hofmeyer. It gave every consideration to Kruger's bogus proposals. It worked at the idea of commissions of enquiry. It made Milner's position almost untenable, in that the loyalists he had rallied together effectively for the first time after years of disillusionment grew daily more convinced, as delay followed delay, that the Home Government was only looking for a face-saving pretext to back down before Boer intransigence and leave its loyal supporters once more in the lurch. This was what Milner himself above all minded. The chorus of abuse from the Boers left him unmoved, though it must, humanly, have added to the strain.

Towards the end of July he was writing to Mr. Rendel: 'Of course, you would think I should mind the attacks. I don't. Frightful as has been the strain of the last 2 months, the abuse, which is loudest here of course (the rebels are just frantic), does not touch me. I am worn with anxiety to do the best, and every turn of the game presents a new responsibility. . . . But though the responsibility weighs heavily, the howling affects me not a whit. You see, there is this great *per contra*. Loyal British S. Africa has risen from its long degradation and stands behind me to a man with an enthusiasm which has not been known since before Majuba.'

And then, in a poignantly revealing phrase, which in a single sentence demolishes the whole conception of Milner as the cold, remote administrator: 'It is a great thing to be, even for a few brief days and weeks, *the leader of a people*, possessing their unbounded confidence.'

The voice of Milner of Balliol, of Toynbee Hall, of the crusading *Pall Mall Gazette*, suddenly rings clearly above the grey fabric of proconsular discretion—only to subside into the dogged determination of the man of immense affairs, hagridden by his care for his country's good name: 'Of course England may give us away—probably will—not from cowardice but from simple ignorance of the situation and the easy-going belief that you have only to be very kind and patient and magnanimous, and *give away your friends to please your enemies*, in order to make the latter love you for ever. She may give us away.

It is the last time she will have the chance. . . .' And finally, in a
postscript, he remembers his debt to Chamberlain, and states it
categorically: '. . . P.S.—Joe has stuck to me *magnificently*. If he
throws me over after all, or, worse still, retreats under a garbled
version of my advice to him, I shall know it is only because he
cannot help it.'

He was always remembering his debt to 'Joe'. Years later,
after the war, we find him writing after one of his tremendous
fulminations against 'the system' (which we shall come to in due
course): 'I never, even to myself, criticise Joe without hastily
adding, "but it is not *his* fault". One is so grateful for greatness
anywhere. It is a sort of *lèse-majesté* of the worst description to
undermine it.'

They certainly tried each other in these critical months:
Chamberlain with the uncomprehending British public on his
back, Milner with the South Africans with their impatient
'*il faut en finir*' on his. But they kept together, and meanwhile, in
the midst of his other duties, Milner did his utmost to support his
Chief in his battles at home, writing long and elaborate letters to
the Liberal leaders explaining his actions in a way in which another
man would have disdained to explain them, filled only with a
determination to help Chamberlain unite the country. A letter
addressed to Sir Edward Grey, which is a masterpiece of diplomatic art and must have cost him much precious time to compose,
ends with the candid expression of his conviction:

> I should like you to feel sure that if the rupture comes, it will not
> be from any spirit of Jingoism in me. But the position is extremely
> bad. We must do something substantial to improve the position of
> our clients, or lose all reputation and political influence, even in what
> will be nominally British South Africa. Such a result must, in my
> opinion, be avoided at any cost, even the cost of war, though I am
> fully alive to the risks, and should not except in the last resort con-
> template it with anything but aversion. Meanwhile the increase of
> our forces here must not be regarded as involving war, but rather as
> diminishing the chance of it. A *very expensive* precaution doubtless,
> but after all what is a million or two to Great Britain if it saves the
> situation in South Africa? It may be a serious matter for the High

Commissioner who has brought about its expenditure. But I don't care so much about *him*.

His arguments bore fruit, and the pains he had taken were not in vain. Immediately after war had finally come, Sir Edward Grey was to write to him:

> ... It is only fair to send you a line to say that in my opinion the end has justified the view you have taken of the South African question from the beginning. We are in for a very serious business, but it is better that it should be faced and had out now than deferred by further negotiations, which I am convinced would have been futile. ... I still think the criticisms in my last letter hold good, but they do not touch the main issue of whether we are right or wrong in this war, and of whether it could have been avoided or not. That is all that really matters, and about that I am quite clear now. ...

During all these months the Treasury and the War Office had been slowly moved to action. Reinforcements had been made to the garrisons of Cape Town and Natal, though still on an insufficient scale, and further troops were on the way. But the state of readiness in the Transvaal was far advanced, as a result of the intensive accumulation of military stores begun even before Milner's arrival in South Africa and fiercely accelerated during the last year of peace. The Boers were now ready to sweep the British out of South Africa. With a final twist of dishonesty in which Kruger proclaimed that the British Government had indeed agreed to accept a limited offer of franchise for British settlers, so qualified and hedged about as to be worthless—a statement totally devoid of truth—only to go back on their word, Kruger gave out his ultimatum, backed by the Government of the Orange Free State, which, until the last moment, played a highly equivocal role.

On October 9th, 1899, Milner received from the British agent in Pretoria the following telegram:

> I have just received a Note from State Secretary in which, after reciting the reasons which have led Government S.A.R. to take this step, they ask H.M. Government to give them four assurances: First—That all points of difference be settled by Arbitration or by peaceful means to be agreed upon. Second—That the troops on the

borders of the Republic be instantly withdrawn. Third—That all increase of troops arrived since June 1st in South Africa be sent back to the sea coast, with an assurance that they will be removed from South Africa within a time to be agreed upon with the Government of the S.A.R. . . . Fourth—that H.M. Troops which are now on the sea shall not be landed in any part of South Africa.

Government S.A.R. urges an affirmative answer to these four questions not later than 5 p.m. on Wednesday, October 11th. Should no favourable answer be received within that interval, Government S.A.R. will regard action of H.M. Government as a formal declaration of war.

On October 10th Milner was instructed to inform the Government of the South African Republic that

Her Majesty's Government have received with great regret the peremptory demands of the Government of the South African Republic. . . . The conditions demanded by the Government of the South African Republic are such as Her Majesty's Government deem it impossible to discuss.

Chapter Twelve

RECONSTRUCTION AND DEFEAT

THE WAR WAS fought and won, laboriously and at unnecessary cost, and after a display of initial incompetence on the part of the War Office which was to make its name a by-word for decades to come. For Milner this war was only the prelude to the real task ahead: the re-fashioning of South Africa as a fully articulated and key component of the Imperial design. He had done all that a man could do, first to by-pass war by negotiation; then, again vainly, to persuade the British Government to shock the Boers out of their complacency by an unequivocal display of resolution; finally, and still vainly, to ensure that when war came we should be well equipped to fight it. Thanks to Chamberlain, he had at last succeeded in bringing round British public opinion; and he had won the blessing of Sir Edward Grey, the distinguished Liberal leader. His battle had been arduous in the extreme, and he had fought it very much single-handed. In addition to his more public troubles he had had to cope with too many burdens in South Africa itself; not only in the form of a disloyal Ministry, which hampered his preparations at every turn (and continued to hamper him throughout the first period of the war), but also, through nine extraordinary months, in the form of his own Deputy and Commander-in-Chief, General Butler, whose eccentricities have already been briefly recorded. It was not until the belated arrival of Lord Roberts to take over the losing cause after Buller's disastrous campaigns that Milner was able to relax. His diplomatic forbearance during the early disasters was exemplary: he had handed over to the soldiers, and, for better or for worse, he gave them his support. But the strain was severe, and the more so because he had so long warned his Government against precisely the sort of thing that happened. When Roberts arrived he permitted himself a sigh of relief: 'I feel at least that we shan't be shot sitting now!' And in some of his private letters he shows clearly enough what he felt.

What an awful show-up it has been [he wrote to Lord Selborne]. Granted we have all made mistakes, what would they really have mattered, but for that *avalanche of military incompetence*, which has nearly swept the Empire away? And what is the disease really? Do you know? Splendid men, splendid officers—and so many things, mobilisation, sea and railway transport, commissariat, *admirably done*. It is not as if the thing was altogether rotten. There is much that is excellent. But the *central machinery* and the *chosen leaders* ... was there ever such a series of mis-selections? The extraordinary thing is that for frank criticism of one another, I know of no set of men equal to our *haute armée*. And yet, when it comes to business, there is the most ridiculous fetish-worship of seniority and positive pusillanimity about the removal of admitted failures.

His main thought, however, even in the blackest days, was for the grand reconstruction, to which in his eyes the war was simply an inevitable and tragic prelude. Already in November he was discussing the future with Sir Percy Fitzpatrick in a letter marked 'Very Confidential' and dated November 28th, 1899:

... It seems ill-omened to talk of eventual settlement when things are in such an awful mess. . . . Still, it must have an end, and that end must be our victory. So though it may be premature, it is still necessary to think what to do with it. One thing is quite evident. The *ultimate* end is a self-governing white Community, supported by *well-treated* and *justly governed* black labour from Cape Town to Zambesi. There must be one flag, the Union Jack, but under it equality of races and languages. Given *equality* all round, English must prevail, though I do not think, and do not wish, that Dutch should altogether die out. I think, though all South Africa should be *one Dominion* with a common government dealing with Customs, Railways, and Defence, perhaps also with Native policy, a considerable amount of freedom should be left to the several States. But although this is the ultimate end it would be madness to attempt it at once. There must be an interval to allow the British population of the Transvaal to return and increase, and the mess to be cleared up, before we can apply the principle of self-government to the Transvaal. . . .

He went on to discuss the problems of finance, and came to the conclusion that, though difficult to overcome, financial problems could not for long 'be a stumbling-block to a country so rich as the Transvaal. The ordinary cost of administration (without Mausers and Creusot guns and 23,000,000 rounds, and corruption, and Secret Service) will be capable of great reduction. . . .'

How long the period of unrepresentative government may last [he went on], I cannot say. I, for one, would be for shortening it as much as possible, but not before a loyal majority is assured. As for the Boer himself, provided I am once sure of having broken his political predominance, I should be for leaving him the greatest amount of individual freedom. First beaten, then fairly treated, and not too much worried on his own 'plaats' in his own conservative habits, I think he will be peaceful enough. It is the interested and intriguing outsider who has stirred him up to all this mischief. . . . I pray for a decisive result. A patch up would be awful. But a decisive result means a tremendous and sustained effort on the part of the British people. . . .

Those, in outline, were Milner's war aims, conceived before the battle began and held to in all their moderation through the heat and fury. Only two things ever stirred him to serious alarm: any rumour that the British Government were prepared to concede full self-government after a short military occupation, and any signs of faltering in the 'tremendous and sustained effort'. It was here that he had his most anxious conflict with Kitchener, to whom the cause owed so much, after Roberts had handed over and during the dismal, long-drawn-out period of sporadic warfare known as the 'pacification', with its horrible accompaniment of concentration camps for women and the burning of farms. It was this period, of course, which was later to fill so many Englishmen with shame and fatally blur their appreciation of the real significance of the war. Milner, as High Commissioner, was a helpless spectator of events he bitterly deplored. From the declaration of war he had handed over to the military, restraining himself from interference or condemnation even when things were at their worst. Now the military were still in charge: the war was still in being, and, without quarrelling with Kitchener, Milner could do nothing.

Even more to the point, as Milner saw it, deeply concerned as he was for the future of South Africa as a whole, were Kitchener's highly personal methods of trying to jump the Boers into surrender, regardless of what happened afterwards. For Kitchener was not interested in the political future of South Africa. He was a soldier of genius. He wanted to shut down and have done with this war which was no longer a war, and get away to India, where there was work to be done of the kind he understood. Everything was subordinated to this end. In his natural and overbearing impatience he would have resorted to any means to trick or stampede the Boers into final submission, regardless of the inevitable reaction when the trickery was discovered. Milner did not quarrel with Kitchener, and he prided himself on this. He recognised his greatness and was conscious of its spell. He was also determined to use all his diplomacy in order to preserve a united front. But the whole outlook and approach of the two men were diametrically opposed, and in letters to Lady Edward Cecil which expose the potentially dramatic conflict, both contrasting characters are most vividly illumined in a sort of *tableau vivant* of mutual incomprehension held in check by mutual respect. Even when he has decided that he cannot possibly work constructively with Kitchener and must simply give him his head and hope for the best, Milner finds himself still fascinated by the character and ability of that extraordinary genius.

> Kitchener will be impossible for me to work with, I can see [he writes], as he is absolutely autocratic and observes no compact. But I don't mind that, *if only he will end the war.* I am quite willing to lie low and let my administratorship be a farce, until the country is pacified, if there is only progress in that direction. And I shall know that he wants to go as soon as he can—therefore I shall just possess my soul in patience till he has finished the rough work in his own strong way and not interfere with him. My only fear is that he may make promises to people, to get them to surrender, which will be embarrassing afterwards to fulfil, and which, if he stayed, he would merrily break. . . . It will not be quite so easy for me to break them.

That was dated December 27th, 1900. A year later, on January 31st, 1902, he was writing: '. . . The stories of differences between

Lord K. and me are subsiding, I think. It is most important that they should subside. The differences are there—not personal but political—but only harm and the weakening of my hand could result from their being talked about.

'Besides I do admire him in his own line. He is fearfully wrong-headed sometimes but he is always *homme serieux*, practising himself, and enforcing upon others, the highest standard of *workmanlike* strenuousness, indefatigable industry and iron perseverance.

'Great qualities these in a wishy-washy world.'

By May of that year his attitude had hardened. On May 11th he wrote from Johannesburg:

> . . . I think [Kitchener's policy] fatally wrong, [his] methods are —no 'think' about this—very crooked. I continue to admire many things about him—indeed he is very near greatness, I think . . .
>
> It would be a simple solution just to let K. make his peace in his own damnable way, provided he would stay to carry out the settlement. There would be some sense in this, for he would not have the least scruple in breaking faith with the Boers and so getting rid of awkward promises and half-promises which he keeps on trying to make, and in which he will involve me and the great Downing Street Jelly-Fish if he can.

And finally, on May 20th, just before the signing of peace, a peace which turned out to be a good deal better than Milner had feared ('That is to say, I have eliminated about 60 per cent of the preposterous demands of the Boers, and, as far as I can make out from messages at present being deciphered, "Joe" is busy at his end knocking off 20 per cent more. This is not so bad, *if you will go into "negotiations"* with a beaten enemy, who are the greatest bluffers in this mortal world'), he wrote: '. . . One thing I am rather proud about, is that I *haven't* quarrelled with K. over all this. No doubt he is as sick of me as I am eternally sick of him. But we manage to get on decently in our personal relations. Of course his being a strong man makes it easier. His personal impact is great. I am not very influenceable in that sort of way, but I am conscious of him deflecting me at times a little from my course, *against* my judgement. . . .'

How deeply fascinated Milner was by this exactly opposed and superlatively confident character is shown in two lines from an earlier letter, before the peace negotiations brought their differences to a state of suppressed crisis: 'I get on excellently with K. . . . I like the total absence of cant, the *clearness of vision*, and the immense strenuousness of his character. He may deceive others. I don't think he deludes himself. He *has not got* the "lie in the soul".'

Peace was finally signed at Vereeniging on May 31st, 1902. On June 28th Chamberlain wrote to Milner telling him that he was to be 'advanced to the position of a Viscount of the United Kingdom'. But the work for which Milner asked to be remembered lay before him: 'What I should prefer to be remembered by is the tremendous effort subsequent to the war, not only to repair its ravages, but to restart these colonies on a higher plane of civilisation than they had ever previously attained.'

The story of the reconstruction is an epic in itself. It has no place in this study, because it does nothing but reflect Milner's genius for far-seeing and energetic administration on which everyone, including his worst enemies, has always been agreed. Indeed, the achievements of these tremendous five years have, paradoxically, perhaps done more than anything to distort the true picture of Milner's qualities and to obscure his greatness as a statesman and a thinker. That Milner had greatness nobody has ever dared to deny. How, then, can his greatness be reconciled with the picture of an aloof and unimaginative proconsul who blundered, by sheer obstinacy, into the most disreputable war in British history?—this being the picture offered by his enemies and too easily accepted by all opposed to the Imperial idea, who never troubled to look at the man for themselves. The answer was at hand: admit that Milner was a great administrator and deny him all other qualities. Emphasise his administrative achievements in South Africa, picture him as a supreme civil servant, and suggestion does its work: how can a born civil servant know anything of handling men?

And so the manifold reconstruction of South Africa is freely admitted, and people look no further—not realising, perhaps, that administration on this scale called for qualities not found in the make-up of a great departmental chief. He set himself not merely to getting South Africa out of the mess the war had made of it, but into developing it farther and more rapidly than anyone had yet dreamed, and encouraging the growth of a British population firmly rooted in prosperity, so that when the time for self-government should come, the new colonies, or dominions, no matter how they were to be called, should naturally and of their own accord range themselves behind the British idea at its best and most constructive. The basis of this new prosperity was to be the gold of the Rand, which must be developed swiftly and intelligently—not only to provide finance, but also to attract new settlers who would have to be fed and so create an incentive for the rationalisation of agriculture. The gold-fields were seen not as an end in themselves, but only as a beginning, and, properly based, the country would thrive in a community of industry and agriculture long after the gold was finished. To increase the agricultural yield in a land of backward farming and poor soil immense schemes for irrigation and communications were drawn up, with a vision and on a scale which were not to be surpassed until the great Russian and American projects much later in the century. These plans for scientific farming, irrigation and afforestation were all to be abandoned, with the rest of Milner's ideas, when the Liberal Government of 1906 so heedlessly reversed his policies.

It was during this period of reconstruction, which began even before the war itself was over, that the figure of Milner became the magnet for the most able and spirited young men of a whole generation, who came to form a sort of commando, unprecedented in the history of the Empire, of devoted lieutenants—the celebrated Kindergarten. These, when Milner finally left South Africa, loaded with honours and with the worst of his task behind him, remained loyal to his ideas and, under their new chief, Lord Selborne, continued as best they could, and in spite of every obstacle put in their way by an anti-Imperialist government at home, to salvage all that could be salvaged from the wreckage of Milner's hopes.

He came home in 1905. 'I am proud', he wrote in a letter to Mrs. Chapin, 'of the fact that any services I may have rendered, or tried to render, in South Africa, have resulted in leaving me a poorer man than I was when I went out there, and I should like to feel that, as far as South Africa is concerned, the balance will always remain on that side. In view of the particular kind of calumny by which the British cause in that country is always assailed, this seems to me of great importance. . . .'

He, and South Africa with him, had come a long way since the first days of the war when he had written to Miss Bertha Synge:

> . . . One can only hang on grimly and hope for better things. The state of this Colony is awful. It simply *reeks with treason*. I have a sad satisfaction in thinking that at least I did not malign people. I was so abused at one time by the ignorant and always befooled British sentimentalists for saying that there was a serious amount of disaffection in the Colony, that at times I began to wonder whether I had not been unjust to these 'simple peasants'. And now! Well! We shall worry through somehow. . . . I am sustained by my own belief in the soundness of the wholly misunderstood cause in which we are fighting. It is war of liberation—from the rule of the Mauser.

Just over five years later he could say farewell, not only to Cape Colony and Natal, but to all South Africa in these terms:

> The question as I see it, the question of the future of the Empire, is a race, a close race, between the many influences manifestly making for disruption, and the growth of a great but as yet imperfectly realised conception.
>
> The words 'Empire' and 'Imperial' are perhaps in some respects unfortunate. They seem to suggest domination, ascendancy, the rule of a superior State over vassal States; but, as they are the only words available, we must make the best of them, and try to raise them in the scale of language by giving them a new significance. When we who call ourselves Imperialists talk of the British Empire, we think of a group of States, all independent in their own local concerns, but all united for the defence of their own common interests and the development of a common civilisation; united, not in an alliance, for alliances can be made and unmade, and are never more than nominally lasting—but in a permanent organic union. Of such a union the dominions of our Sovereign as they

exist today, are, we fully admit, only the raw material. Our ideal is still distant, but we deny that it is either visionary or unattainable. . . .

And again:

> If you believe in me, defend my works when I am gone. . . . I shall live in the memories of the people here, if I live at all, in connection with the great struggle to keep this country within the limits of the British Empire. Certainly I engaged in the struggle with all my might, because I was from head to foot one mass of glowing conviction in the rightness of our cause. But a frightfully destructive conflict of that kind is at best a sad business to look back upon. I should prefer to be remembered for the tremendous effort, wise or unwise in various particulars, made after the war, not only to repair its ravages, but also to restart the new Colonies on a far higher plane of civilisation than they had ever previously attained.

That was in March 1904. In February 1906 this extraordinary man, who had left Africa in a chorus of praise, loaded with the 370,000 signatures to an address recording the highest appreciation of his services to South Africa and the Empire, was now hounded by the Government of his own country, on the edge of being publicly censured, and, as a statesman, reduced to pleading that the white settlers who had made South Africa should not be totally abandoned:

> I do most urgently want to ask His Majesty's Government this most immediate, urgent, practical question. What are you going to do in the Orange River Colony about the new British settlers upon the land—those, I mean, who are Government tenants—about the British teachers in Government schools, about the constabulary, about the officials, high or low, but especially the humbler of them, who have served you with so much devotion during these last arduous years? Are you just going to hand them over like that without any further concern as to what may happen to them. . . ?
>
> Remember, this is no case of gradual constitutional development. It is the case of a sudden revolution. Loyalty to the old system will be a black mark against a man under the new. The Government must surely feel that, if it is a question between the grant of full responsible government and this country keeping faith, they should choose the latter. . . .

The Government, of course, felt nothing of the kind. And this is a thing for which the Liberals should not be exclusively blamed. As we all know now, given a choice between standing up for a friend or sacrificing him as a gesture of appeasement to the enemy, all British Governments of whatever colour invariably choose the second course. Shouts of self-congratulation drown the cries of the victims; but the enemy is not appeased. We remember Milner's great despatch on appeasement from the first days of his South African appointment: 'It is no ·use being conciliatory if people think you are only conciliatory because you are afraid. . . .'

About his own personal trials he had little to say, and what he did say was concerned less with his own suffering than with the principle of ingratitude and indiscriminate abuse for party ends as it might affect the future well-being of the country.

He referred to it in his Empire Day speech, expressing his pride and gratification in the 'deluge of friendly letters which had poured in, quite unexpectedly, from all over the world, and from all parties at home'.

> And the meaning of it all I take to be this, that there is a strong instinct in the heart of the British nation to treat its public servants with a certain broad generosity—an instinct which especially resents their being prejudiced in any way by the accidents and exigencies of party warfare. And that instinct, my Lords and gentlemen, is a great asset. It makes for the nation being faithfully and fearlessly served. Of course, nobody desires that the servants of the State—I am speaking of those whose offices do not change with changes of party—should on that account be free from criticism, or, if need be, from censure. But the general feeling is, and it is a right feeling, that their work and service should be judged as a whole, that allowance should be made for their difficulties, and that the public should not be extreme to mark what is done amiss when it is neither possible nor desirable to be constantly marking every successful discharge of an arduous duty.

Chapter Thirteen

THE VOTE OF CENSURE

HE CAME HOME not only to see the ruin of his vision, but also to receive public humiliation—or what was intended to be public humiliation—at the hands of his enemies: that is to say, at the hands of the enemies of the British Empire, for as a man he had no enemies. It was commonly believed that his absence from the general political scene for the next ten years was due to bitterness at the notorious vote of censure, but nothing could be farther from the truth. He was not bitter. And his mind had been made up long before, as we shall shortly see: politics, as such, were not for him. He took his seat in the House of Lords and there fought hard for many causes which he had at heart, labouring ceaselessly behind the scenes. He reappeared on the floodlit public stage at Lloyd George's urgent invitation, in 1916, not because he wanted office, but because there was a clear-cut job to be done, which he thought he could do.

Nor did he sulk in his tent when, for him, the worst was allowed to happen in South Africa. He fought against it while he could, and afterwards he threw himself heart and soul into helping his late colleagues and successors to make the best of a bad job. He was fighting in 1906, his eloquence only checked a little by the very real fear of provoking the enemies of his cause into action even more extreme—not against him, but against the future of South Africa within the Empire. As he himself observed in his Empire Day speech: 'My difficulty has always been how to warn the Government and the nation of the dangers ahead, of some of which Ministers themselves appeared at one time quite unaware, without stirring up those, who were pushing the Government into extreme courses, to a yet greater activity of mischief. But there was a time at which silence would have been, so at least it seemed to me, little short of crime.'

The great fighting speeches were made in February and March, 1906, after the Liberal landslide: one before, one just after the Commons vote of censure with which an anti-Imperialist Government celebrated its heady triumph. He had, apart from the Chinese labour question, two points to make, and he made them with such vigour and clarity, forming a case so unanswerable, that the fact that the Government was uninfluenced by them is as striking a commentary as one would easily find on the defencelessness of reason in face of undisciplined emotion, which has only to transform itself into hysteria to sweep everything before it:

> I think it was the late Lord Salisbury [he said] who once pithily described the situation by saying that the only bond between the Mother Country and a colony with responsible government was the bond of affection. But what if that, the only bond, is lacking? And in this case how can any reasonable man expect it already to exist?
>
> Here is a colony, three-quarters of whose inhabitants have been at war with you up to less than four years ago, a war that was fought with the utmost determination to the bitter end. It is true that they have been treated since then with a generosity which I believe has no parallel in history, that everything has been done, both to restore their material prosperity and to spare their susceptibilities, and that this treatment has not been without effect. . . . But though all that is very satisfactory as far as it goes, it does not amount to anything that by the wildest stretch of imagination could be called affection for British institutions or the British Empire.

He went on to show how the influential Boers, far from becoming reconciled, 'have from the very outset devoted themselves to thwarting the policy of reconciliation and to keeping alive by every means in their power the bitterest memories of the war', and that these, under self-government forming a large majority, would, slowly and quietly, constitutionally and without sensation, steadily

> get rid of the British officials, the British teachers, the bulk of the British settlers, and any offensive British taint which may cling to the Statute-book or the administration.
>
> I can quite understand that from the point of view of what are

known as the pro-Boers such a result is eminently desirable. They thought the war was a crime, the annexation a blunder, and they think today that the sooner you can get back to the old state of things the better. . . . . What I cannot understand is how any human being, not being a pro-Boer, can regard with equanimity the prospect that the very hand which drafted the ultimatum of October 1899, may within a year be drafting 'Ministers' Minutes' for submission to a British governor who will have virtually no option but to obey them.

He went on to specify the kind of Minutes that in such circumstances might well be produced for the governor's unwilling signature.

These are not imaginings [he said]. They are just reminiscences. I know what it is to be governor of a self-governing colony, with the disaffected element in the ascendant. I was bitterly attacked for not being sufficiently submissive under the circumstances. Yet even with the least submissive governor, the position is so weak that strange things happen. It was under responsible government, and in the normal working of responsible government, that 1,000,000 cartridges were passed through Cape Colony on the eve of the war, to arm the people who were just going to attack us, and that some necessary cannon were stopped from being sent to a defenceless border town, which directly afterwards was besieged, and which, from want of these cannon, was nearly taken.

The vote of censure, of which so much has been made, caused him far less distress than the reversal of his hopes for South Africa. His friends, and even those who thought they were his enemies, were amazed at his unconcern about his own reputation and the way in which he not only refused to allow that dismal manoeuvre to affect his relations with acquaintances on the other side of the House, but also positively went out of his way to preserve them from embarrassment.

He was unaffected by the Censure not only because all that he had ever said about not caring for himself was the simple truth, but also because he had by then come to his own conclusions about the party game. And this extravagant action was, to him, simply one more confirmation. Had he been the solitary victim, he would not have cared: he knew enough about life and politics to see that there must always be victims and scapegoats, and he was too much of a philosopher to see any reason why he himself should not belong to their company. But he was not the solitary victim. With him went his whole conception of South Africa, of the Empire, of the future of Britain in the world.

It did not, of course, all go in the vote of censure, which was no more than a personal attack on him, scarcely disguised, and obviously moved by the venom and spite of small men infuriated by the success of a great man, who had scorned all their devices and shifts for achieving success and nevertheless triumphed where they had failed. It began with the first attack on Chinese labour and it ended with the sweeping away of the so-called Lyttelton Constitution for South Africa in 1906, before it had even been put into operation.

> Politicians will be politicians [in the words of Mr. Headlam, words all the more telling because of his studied moderation throughout the bulk of his two great volumes]; but in the whole history of party warfare there is not to be found anything more cynical and disgusting than the speeches, backed by banners and cartoons of flogged and fettered Chinamen, by which the anti-Chinese agitation was worked up in Parliament, the Press, the Chapel and the street corner, by right reverend prelates and non-conformist divines, by Hyde Park orators, and right honourable gentlemen who themselves sanctioned similar restrictions on indented labour elsewhere. They were all the more effective, and all the more unforgivable, because they were a deliberate exploitation of one of the most just and generous instincts of the British people.

This was indeed a case in which Milner's distrust of the motives of his opponents, which we have seen at times to have bordered on the extravagant, was justified up to the hilt. The Liberals were going to get the Tories out at the next election. The Liberals were also determined, regardless of the consequences, to wash their hands of South Africa. Chinese labour gave them their cry, and they exploited it with a deliberate cynicism which was proved to have been also blatant when, achieving power, they immediately back-pedalled and passed an act continuing the system for another four years, incidentally, through Mr. Winston

Churchill, giving birth to the notorious phrase: 'a terminological inexactitude' used as a synonym for a lie. The terminological inexactitude was the use of the word 'slavery', deliberate and repeated, withdrawn only after the election, to describe the conditions of the Chinese labourers.

We have already touched on this question of Chinese labour for its value as a sidelight on the way in which Milner's mind worked. There is no need to go into it now at any length. The mines of the Transvaal were working on half-time for lack of native labour. The British were being thrown out of work. Two separate commissions had reported that in order to sustain the country, for whose welfare the war had been fought, coloured labour must be imported. Africa could not provide enough. The system of indentured imported labour was already in use in other parts of the Empire. In 1894 a Liberal Government had sponsored the British Guiana Ordinance for the importation of Indian coolies on a five-year term of indenture. The Liberal Government of 1906, the same one which used the Chinese slavery cry as an aid to power, was to sanction the use of indentured labour in the New Hebrides. The whole point of the Chinese importation was to make possible the increased employment of skilled white labour in the Rand, not, as the agitation claimed, to compete with white labour. In this it achieved its purpose while hedging the coolies with elaborate safeguards and, by guaranteeing their repatriation after the allotted term, avoiding anything that might lead to further racial complications. Milner knew very well that the more extreme Liberals would seek to make party capital out of the scheme. Because of this he was at pains to consult beforehand with the leaders of the Opposition, and to obtain assurances from them, freely given, that those Liberals who had supported him during the war would continue to do so over this matter. Asquith, Grey, and Haldane were among these. Campbell-Bannerman, Lloyd George, and the Little Englanders generally were, of course, openly implacable and on principle against anything at all calculated to strengthen the British position in South Africa.

But as the election drew near, the arrangement, to put it mildly, broke down; and, with the exception of Haldane, all those

Liberals who had promised Milner their support joined in the battle cry. It says a great deal for the Conservative Government of the day, which, on the face of it, was not up to much, that it stood loyally by Milner and gave his detractors as good as they got. '. . . Well, we have had such a time over the Chinese Labour Question,' wrote Lord Goschen, Milner's first chief. 'Such rows and such battles over your body! All your critics became frantic, and I think have damaged themselves by their frightful extravagance. No one worse than the Bishop of Hereford, who was disgracefully violent, and gave me the opportunity of giving him such a dressing as I expect no Bishop has had for years in the House of Lords. . . .'

Milner himself was not in the least apologetic. To Bishop Hamilton Baynes, formerly Bishop of Natal, who had written disassociating himself from the Bishop of Hereford's attack, he replied:

> As for 'slavery', there is no more slavery in this than in a hundred forms of service, based upon free contract—certainly not as much as in ordinary enlistment in the Army. . . . And this country absolutely requires some extraneous help to get along. Without it, there will be a white exodus, and that, of course, means a British exodus. And this, I am perfectly certain, is the reason why Chinese labour is so much opposed. It is the pro-Boers and Little Englanders, who are really at the bottom of the whole business, though they are leading the bulk of their well-meaning fellow-countrymen by the nose. To say that Chinese labour is *a substitution for white labour* is, quite simply, a lie, and those who have raised the clamour know it is a lie, but it has taken in thousands of people. The exact opposite is the truth. Without a substratum of coloured labour, white labour cannot exist here, and when the very rich mines are worked out, the country will return to its primitive barrenness— and to the Boer. And that is the true inwardness of the whole business. . . .

Milner did not believe that the ultimate paradise on earth was to be achieved by City of London adventurers developing the gold-mines of the Rand with the help of Chinese labourers. He believed, as he believed of everything he did in South Africa, that it was the only practical way of moving slowly on in the immense task, which in the end proved too much for the English, of developing South Africa as a vital and all-important part of a federated British Commonwealth which, being on the whole a maturer and less grasping power than any other in the world, might be expected to exercise an influence for stability and peace a little stronger than any other power in the world. He has yet to be proved wrong in this modest assumption.

For the time being he won. The Chinese Labour Ordinance was passed, among the storms described by Lord Goschen, in the spring of 1904. Milner had exactly a year to go in South Africa, and a great deal of that year was taken up by correspondence with the Home Government about his successor and the drafting of the Lyttelton Constitution, which was designed to give a degree of representative government to the Transvaal and the Orange River Colony, the main object of which was to ensure that the coming Liberal Government would have no excuse for sweeping away in one gesture all that had so far been built up. They came to power in the landslide of December 1905, and before the next year was out had censured Milner and given back to the Boers all that we had won. The election was fought largely on the Chinese labour plank, of which the most unscrupulous use was made. But the Conservatives were finished without that. The burning issue was Cheap Food versus Tariffs, which also meant a defeat for a great deal that Milner, still ahead of his times, most firmly stood for. It was not because the Liberals won the election that Milner objected to Imperial affairs being brought into party politics. He would have felt no less strongly about it had they lost. Nor was his abhorrence of the system that threw the greatest and most complicated issues to the mercy of electioneering politicians in the least confined to Great Britain. Indeed, it is safe to say that what he had seen of party feuds in South Africa, feuds which did not in the least affect his own position one way or the other, had had a great deal to do with the development of his conviction. In April 1904 we find him writing to Sir Clinton Dawkins about the elections in South Africa:

... You have had to stir up all the old racial animosities which, under an impartial loyal govt. (not depending on elections, election violence, election dodges and the race hatred which electioneering excites to its highest pitch) would by now have been dying down. At the end of the war there were plenty of Dutchmen who, if they had not been forced at once to side for or against 'the national cause' at the polls, would have been only too glad to live peaceably with their British neighbours under a neutral administration, which would have had no temptation to stir up race animosity and hound English against Dutch. What you have got now, under your blessed responsible Govt., is what every man knowing the country foresaw you must have, i.e. parties, almost equally matched, fighting for power *on the race issue alone*, and the race feud firmly rooted for years, when you had a golden chance of eradicating it. . . .

And in November of the same year to another correspondent:

. . . Personally I have no political interest worth mentioning, except the maintenance of the Imperial connection; and I look upon the future with alarm. The party system at home and in the Colonies seems to me to work for the severance of ties, and that contrary to the desire of our people on both sides. It is a melancholy instance of the manner in which bad political arrangements, lauded to the skies from year's end to year's end as the best in the world, may not only injure the interests, but actually frustrate the desires of the people. I can see no remedy or protection, under present circumstances, except a powerful body of men—and it would have to be very powerful—determined at all times and under all circumstances to vote and work, regardless of every other consideration, against the man or party who played fast and loose with the cause of National Unity. You can be sure that for my own part I shall always do that.

He was already writing in the knowledge of his homecoming. On May 9th, 1904, he was writing to Lyttelton:

It is quite certain, that I should not live 6 weeks with a Radical Government, even if they did not recall me at once, as in their own interests they had better do. Therefore I want to clear *in time for you to appoint my successor*. And, from the purely personal point of view, I want to clear, at latest, in the spring of 1905. Reasons of health are decisive. I may live many years yet. But it is quite certain that, if I am to live as anything but an old crock, I must be taken out of this harness before very long, and turned out to grass for at least a year, perhaps longer. I have medical authority for this, but if there were no such thing as a doctor in the world, I should know it quite well from my own experience. If it was in the public interest that I should go on until I dropped, I should not hesitate. I am 50 and have had a run for my money. But what I will not face is the gradual but certain loss of efficiency, which going on when you are worn out involves.

Balfour thought differently and wanted him to stay, 'like Cromer for an indefinite period'. But in vain. Milner's mind was made up, and soon he was hailing his successor, Lord Selborne, as the greatest possible relief. Soon, too, South Africa suddenly realised what was happening, and 'a hush fell upon the storm of cavillings and criticisms which had recently been pouring upon Milner and his work. Men of all parties suddenly remembered what South Africa owed to him, and realised what he had been doing to lay for them the foundations of a new and national life within the Empire.' Letters and addresses of gratitude and admiration poured in in an overwhelming stream; and in a series of farewell speeches Milner, with a candour reminiscent of Graaf Reinet, outlined his views as to the future of South Africa, summarised what had been done and what remained to be done, and warned his audiences of their shortcomings. Without a trace of rhetoric he held vast audiences spellbound by sheer respect for his courage and his mind. For a short time even the Boers put aside their hatred of him.

But the English Liberals did not. Instead of coming straight home to rest, as he had intended, Milner broke his journey for three months to be with his friend Clinton Dawkins, who was dying in Italy. When he got back there were six months to go to the elections and the landslide, under the edifying cry of 'Slavery under the British Flag', which the new government, through Lord Elgin and Mr. Winston Churchill, hastened to repudiate as soon as it had served their turn. But they had far from finished with Milner, and chance played into their hands. The ill-treatment of a number of Chinese coolies under an unconstitutional regulation led to discussion in the House of Lords in which Milner took on to himself full responsibility for actions performed without his knowledge. It was what the Commons had been waiting for, and on March 21, 1906, two months after achieving power, a formal vote of censure in extravagant terms on Milner personally was put down by Mr. William Byles. The Government could not support this motion as it stood, but, through Mr. Churchill, it moved an amendment to record its condemnation of the flogging of Chinese coolies in breach of the law but refraining 'from passing censure upon individuals'.

The motion was carried by 355 votes to 135, Balfour, Chamberlain, and others coming hotly less to the defence of Milner, who needed no defence, but rather to the defence of the good name of Parliament. The following week the House of Lords recorded 'its high appreciation of the services rendered by Lord Milner to South Africa and the Empire'. On Empire Day, Curzon, Chamberlain and others paid the highest possible tribute to Milner at a banquet attended by a galaxy of the greatest in the land. Milner himself was overwhelmed by letters and telegrams from men of all parties in Great Britain and South Africa expressing their disgust with the Parliamentary exhibition. *Punch* printed its famous cartoon. Alfred Lyttelton, Milner's late chief in the office which he himself had refused, wrote personally: '. . . In the world of shadows I was called your political chief. But in the world of realities you must know that I always thought of you as mine, and that I shall always think of you as a leader. And so I heard with intense pleasure the stately and convincing argument of yesterday, and felt that the truth has already, and will still more potently prevail. . . .'

Milner himself wrote to Lord Roberts: '. . . *I do not care one atom about myself.* The Radical attack has done me no harm, except to bring me a perfect avalanche of letters and telegrams of enthusiastic sympathy, and offers of every sort and kind of thing, by which I am hopelessly embarrassed. *But* the action of the Government and House of Commons must do harm in South Africa, and the Lords can do something to minimise it. This post has brought me the most extraordinary South African correspondence you ever saw. Two things stand out pre-eminent, (1) the awful effect, discouragement everywhere, positive alarm among the scattered British of the Orange River Colony, produced by the King's Speech; (2) the encouragement derived from the House of Lords debate.'

The House of Lords debate was on the King's Speech, through which the new Liberal Government announced its intention of conceding full responsible government to the Transvaal. The Lyttelton Constitution was thus stillborn. When under the new dispensation the Transvaal had its first election early in 1907, the Boers obtained a large majority over the pro-British element, which was divided against itself. Thus, five years after the great struggle which Milner had seen as the first step in the establishment of a new and hopeful order for South Africa under the British Crown, Botha was installed as Prime Minister of the Transvaal and Fischer as Prime Minister of the Orange River Colony. The Cape Dutch followed suit. And on April 17th, 1907, we find Milner writing to Sir H. F. Wilson:

> . . . From my point of view all that has happened during the past eighteen months is wholly deplorable. People here—not only Liberals—seem delighted, and to think themselves wonderfully fine fellows for having given South Africa back to the Boers. I think it all sheer lunacy. But of course, from one point of view, the thing is satisfactory. I used to worry myself sometimes thinking whether this thing could not have been done better, or that had not better have been left undone. But in face of a *volte face* so complete, obviously it would not have made the slightest difference what one did. It was evidently hopeless from the first to try and make a good job of South Africa for the British people. They are not holding on to it, and the only wonder is that even 'Joe' ever managed to get them to make the effort they once did. . . .

PART THREE

THINKER AND IDEALIST

Chapter Fourteen

PAX BRITANNICA

WE SHALL NOT trace the rest of Milner's life in detail. This is not a biography of a great man—he himself shrank from such a memorial, and could never understand what possessed people to write, and read, three-decker monuments to dull and stupid lives while so many great, original and vital men and women fell into oblivion simply because they had never held high office. It was necessary to show his work in South Africa in some detail because it was here that he revealed his true stature and made his reputation; and it was here too that he clashed with that aspect of the British attitude which was to dominate the scene increasingly for years to come. It does no harm for the loudest and most indiscriminate opponents of South African policy today to be shown that they themselves, or their ideological fathers, are directly and solely responsible for the existence of this policy, for better or for worse. At the time of the Boer War it was the grandfather of Seretse Khama who did more than anyone else to save Rhodesia for us, and thus, indirectly, South Africa. And the men who gave up South Africa gave up not only the most true among British loyalists, while driving the rest into the arms of the Dutch, but also the natives, who looked to us for help.

But the rest of Milner's life is less controversial. The African story is enough to show the sort of man he was, and how the work of a great man can be nullified and his very wisdom smothered by political passions of the most irresponsible kind. For there is no doubt at all that, disgusting as the Liberal Government's behaviour was and bitterly as the more responsible leaders came to regret it, some of the mud did stick in the popular mind—at least to the extent of arousing in it an imprecise feeling of uncertainty and distrust.

As far as the leaders were concerned, they knew very well that here was a great man, in a world not replete with great men, who in an emergency could always be called upon in the certain knowledge that he would come forward and do what he was required to do without a trace of rancour. He knew all about emergencies.

> . . . The fun of it is [he wrote at the height of the South African crisis] that everyone of the hundred odd people, whom I have to try and get to co-operate, if the coach is to be dragged out of the mire at all, almost invariably expects that he shall be set to do his own pet job in his own particular manner—otherwise 'he won't play'. Of course this is ridiculous. . . . We have all got to do what is wanted, not what we want. The unreasonableness of the average man, at a time of crisis, is really extraordinary. . . .

When the greater crisis came in 1914 he himself placed no terms on his co-operation. With the outbreak of war he threw himself into the thankless task of organising the nation's manpower, food, and coal supplies. And when his ancient and bitter enemy, Lloyd George, became Prime Minister, he accepted without demur the invitation to join the Inner War Cabinet of five. A job had to be done, and he knew he could do it.

But from 1906 to 1914 there were no jobs to be done to which he could surrender himself entirely. No official jobs, that is to say. For the whole conduct of Imperial affairs was directly opposed to everything he himself believed in. He did not try to obstruct. Once the milk was spilt nobody could have thrown himself more loyally into the work of making do with what was left. He had written in July 1902 when, as we have seen, his thoughts were crystallising into the determination never again to accept public office:

> Well. There it is. As long as I am here, I shall continue to do what I can. But I am not going down to the bottom of the hill to roll that stone up again.
>
> If any man was ever completely and finally cured of anything, I am cured of the least shadow or vestige of a desire to save a province or an Empire for Great Britain *in spite* of *her Govt.* and *people*.
>
> Personally I am happier than I have been for a long time. No man was at heart ever less ambitious, or by nature less of a politician. I

have been forced into prominence by my devotion to a cause. The devotion remains, but it remains as a sentiment merely. As a sane man I realise that I can't swim against a maelstrom of rotten opinion, and I am not going to try. The penalty of the successful statesman is that he is kept so busy that he loses his inner life. The reward of the unsuccessful one—*who has a clear conscience*—is that he can afford to devote himself to pursuits and an existence, which in themselves are deeper, truer and more permanent than the life of the Senate or the Forum.

All this is very serious—sounds, perhaps, a little high-flown. But as it is absolutely sincere, I put it down.

That was written in 1902, before he had been offered and refused the Colonial Office, long before the triumph of his enemies, and at a time when everybody thought of him as standing on the very pinnacle of success. He alone knew better.

And so, he retired. He had refused the Cabinet. He had lost money. He had even refused to accept at the hands of his friends and admirers a country place in which he could settle. He bought the small tumble-down Kentish manor-house of Sturry, which he proceeded to turn into a home. He worked hard in the city for a very modest living, above all as an extremely active director of the Rio Tinto concern. He worked hard for the Rhodes Trust and for the National Service League. And instead of playing party politics he devoted himself heart and soul to rousing the nation and the Empire to face the dangers which lay on all sides.

He did not specify those dangers. That was not his task. It was enough to know that nothing stands still, that the weak are attacked by the strong, that enemies are liable to spring up in unexpected places, driven by ambition, the desire for power, crusading zeal, or sheer economic necessity. But when the stability and endurance of a great power was in question, there was only one enemy to fear, the enemy within, weakening the fabric and making it vulnerable. Defeat the enemy within, whether complacency, inertia, or moral slackness, and the exterior enemy would never materialise. Thus Milner's eyes were turned inwards, not outwards; and all his speeches and writing to the end of his life were concerned not with the evocation of

F.I.—9

exterior perils, but with the domestic health of Great Britain and her Empire. If this was allowed to deteriorate there would always be foes to profit by it, and it hardly mattered whether they were white or black or yellow, Teuton, Latin, Slav, Mongol or Negro. Thus, too, so intent did he become on the great problem which dominated his whole life increasingly—how the Empire was to survive in a world inimical to the indefinite survival of empires— that he overlooked the detail. Thus, while he may have under-rated the imminence of the German challenge before 1914, during that very period he was ceaselessly, and without a thought for his own popularity, agitating for the introduction of con-scription, so that the country might be well prepared to meet trouble from whatever quarter, when it came. He was, in a word, so acutely preoccupied with the evils which, by taking thought, we could avoid that he had little attention left for the evils arising from the conduct of others outside our effective control. But he was always ready to meet a threat, even though he might not see the direction from which it was coming; and the moment it mater-ialised he was instinctively and effortlessly making the dispositions of a genius to counter it. Thus, in a flash, when he visited the Western Front to find means of stopping the gap caused by the German breakthrough of March 1918, he made up his mind that there must be a unified command and that the man to hold it was Foch. His whole life, however, was spent in trying to create a state of affairs in which threats could not be made. His ideal, as we have seen, was the British Empire—not as it was, but as it one day might be.

For him Imperialism was patriotism, and to be a British patriot appeared to him the best and most practical way—indeed, the only practical way—of becoming a good citizen of the world. Everything followed from that, so that the Imperialism of Lord Milner had nothing to do with empire-building for the sake of empire-building. It was a way of life dictated by the terms of life to an overpopulated island which could not survive without the most intimate connections with other parts of the globe. For him Imperialism did not mean grabbing new territories. It meant the development of a policy at home and abroad designed to fit the

British for their great responsibilities—and opportunities. Thus, if the defeat of the Boer tyranny was one aspect of Imperialism, another was the abolition of slums and sweated labour at home, which weakened the race and made it unfit to discharge its most exacting functions.

Or, in his own words, from the preface to the collection of his speeches, published in 1913, called *The Nation and Empire*:

> . . . no great movement of the human spirit has ever been more completely misunderstood. But the misconception of it is being gradually overcome. Imperialism as a political doctrine has been represented as something tawdry and superficial. In reality it has all the depth and comprehensiveness of a religious faith. Its significance is moral even more than material. It is a mistake to think of it as principally concerned with 'painting the map red'. There is quite enough painted red already. It is not a question of a couple of hundred thousand square miles more or less. It is a question of preserving the unity of a great race, of enabling it, by maintaining that unity, to develop freely on its own lines, and to continue to fulfil its distinctive mission in the world.

He spoke a good deal about race in his later years, a word now suspect. The question of race was one which exercised him a great deal. His concern was the natural reflection of his own experience which had brought home to him the racial question in the sharpest possible way, both in Egypt and South Africa. He was in no position to pretend, even if he had so desired, that some peoples are not more fitted to rule than others; and to anybody who had asked why any people, even the fittest, should rule at all, he would have replied that this begged the question: in the world as constituted, there were in fact rulers and ruled, and if the fittest abdicated, then the less fit would walk in. This holds good as far as the eye can see. If we had a world government tomorrow, that government would inevitably be dominated by the strongest power in the world—by the U.S.A., that is to say, or by Russia. Its maintenance would depend absolutely on the force of the strongest power or group of powers, who would thus in practice be the rulers of a barely disguised world empire. That is not, of course, in itself an argument against world government.

Milner believed with passion that the British possessed certain qualities which other peoples lacked. We have seen enough to know that no Englishman has ever looked upon his compatriots with a more critical eye. But he still believed, and his declaration of faith in British Imperialism was made after long and bitter and humiliating experience of British muddling and irresponsibility at its worst.

'I am a Nationalist and not a Cosmopolitan' [he wrote in his notebook shortly before his death, under the heading, 'A Key to my Position']. This seems to be becoming more and more the real dividing line of parties.

A Nationalist is not a man who necessarily thinks his nation better than others, or is unwilling to learn from others. He does think that his duty is to his own nation and its development. He believes that this is the law of human progress. . . .

I am a British (indeed primarily an English) Nationalist. If I am also an Imperialist, it is because the destiny of the English race, owing to its insular position and long supremacy at sea, has been to strike fresh roots in distant parts of the world.

My patriotism knows no geographical but only racial limits. I am an Imperialist and not a Little Englander, because I am a British Race patriot. It seems unnatural to me—I think it is impossible from my point of view—to lose interest in and attachment to my fellow countrymen because they settle across the sea. It is not the soil of England, dear as it is to me, which is essential to arouse my patriotism, but the speech, the traditions, the spiritual heritage, the principles, the aspirations of the British race. They do not cease to be *mine* because they are transplanted—my horizon must widen, that is all.

But though he spoke of race in this way he entertained no quasi-mystical theories as to its meaning or validity. It was a convenient word for an irrefutable fact, and will be again when Goebbels and Rosenberg are forgotten.

But what do I mean by the British race? [he asked in his preface to *The Nation and Empire*]. I mean all the peoples of the United Kingdom and their descendants in other countries under the British flag. The expression may not be ethnologically accurate. The inhabitants of England, Scotland and Ireland are of various stocks ... And yet to speak of them collectively as the British race is not only convenient, but it is in accordance with broad political facts. Community of language and institutions, and centuries of life together under one sovereignty, have not indeed obliterated differences, but have super-added bonds, which are more than artificial, which make them in the eyes of the world, if not always in their own, a single nation, and which it will be found impossible to destroy.

His championship of the British, as a race, or people, fit to rule, was equally empirical: 'Imperialism is something wider than "Anglo-Saxondom" or even than 'Pan-Britannicism". The power of incorporating alien races, without trying to disintegrate them or to rob them of their individuality, is characteristic of the British Imperial system. . . .'

He was aware of the dangers of 'this principle of boundless tolerance' and could see it being carried much too far. But when all was said, 'This broad inclusiveness is one of the great secrets of the success of British rule. It is part of our moral capital as a nation, and gives us a title higher than mere force to the position which we occupy in the world.'

It was a title which some others quite patently lacked:

It is peculiar to the British Empire among Empires, and to the British nation as an Empire-building race. Whether this is due to some original quality in the race itself—to its own composite character—or merely to the teachings of experience, I need not here attempt to determine. I am not concerned with the causes of the fact, but with the fact itself and its consequences. It was not thus that Prussia dealt with her Polish subjects, or Russia with the Poles and Finns. It was not thus that the early Dutch settlers in South Africa treated the Huguenots who took refuge among them. They stamped out the language and nationality of these fellow-Protestants and forced them all into their own mould. No doubt we could not, if we would, deal with the Dutch in like fashion. But it is equally true that we would not if we could. We have never attempted it. Respect for their language and individuality, equality of citizenship between the white races, have been our principles from the first. Not only has this attitude become, in South Africa as elsewhere, a fundamental tenet of British Imperialism, but it is rooted in the character of the British race. And if it is true, as it certainly is, that the spirit of liberality and tolerance, of respect not only for personal freedom but for racial individuality, is essential to the preservation of the Empire, it is equally true that that spirit finds its firmest supporters in the British element of the population. When the British flag was hauled down in the Transvaal in 1881, the principle of equal citizenship disappeared with it, and the spirit of uni-racial dominance and exclusiveness took its place.

Believing all this, and it would indeed be very hard, if not impossible, to refute it, he drew the inescapable conclusion: the race had to be upheld and its unity preserved. And this was not easy.

It is true that this wide dispersion of the British race has certain great advantages—it has given it a unique range of experience, and the control of an unrivalled wealth and variety of material resources. But this dispersion is at the same time a source of weakness, and a source of danger, for it is owing to it, and to it almost alone, that the problem of maintaining political unity is so difficult.

It was owing, in a word, to the accident of British expansion in far-scattered places: to the fact that this island has no frontiers but the sea. For Rome in the past, for Russia and America more recently, the problem of unifying scattered elements from a remote and peripheral base never existed. For them nothing was easier than to expand gradually outwards, absorbing alien races step by step and consolidating their gains almost unconsciously as they secured them. From the point of view of the Russian, the Georgians and Armenians of the Caucasus, the Kalmuks, the Tadjiks, the Uzbeks, Khirgizes and all the rest of their Asiatic Empire were backward tribes to be coerced or absorbed into neutrality, foreign bodies inhabiting the great Russian mainland. But from the point of view of all these unfortunate peoples, and a score of others, the Russian colonisers appeared as conquerors and oppressors, no less remote from their way of life than the British from the South Sea Islanders, and a great deal more harsh and overbearing. The British Empire alone among all modern Empires, because of its maritime origins, stood out, for all the world to see, including the

British themselves, for what it was, and found itself confronted with a problem of maintaining unity harder to solve than any in the history of the world:

> Indeed it is only 'the shrinkage of the world', due to the triumphs of mechanical science, which has rendered the solution of that problem possible at all. But now that a solution is possible, the failure to find it would be incredible folly and a huge disaster. That communities of the same origin, the same language, the same political and social structure, the same type of civilisation, with all that they have to cherish, to develop, and to defend in common, should fail to stand together, and should, owing to that failure, run the risk of falling severally under alien domination, would be as unnatural as suicide.
>
> And like suicide, it would mean dereliction of duty. For the British race has become responsible for the peace and order and the just and humane government of three or four hundred millions of people, who, differing as widely as possible from one another in other respects, are all alike in this, that, from whatever causes, they do not possess the gift of maintaining peace and order for themselves. Without our control their political condition would be one of chaos, as it was for centuries before that control was established. The *Pax Britannica* is essential to the maintenance of civilised conditions of existence among one-fifth of the human race.

And again:

> The decisive factor in the case is the question of time. It is inconceivable that the British race, which, with all its faults, has never been lacking in fundamental sanity, should throw away the advantages of its unique position in the world, of its hold on five continents, of its possession of economic resources more vast and varied than any that have ever before fallen under a single control, when once it is fully realised what that position means. But its meaning is not easily brought home to a number of separate democracies, living at a distance from one another, confronted with very different local problems, and each naturally absorbed in its own local affairs.

Chapter Fifteen

THE BANE OF 'THE SYSTEM'

WE SET OUT to find, among other things, why a man of such tremendous gifts did not rise to dominate his age. The reason should now be apparent. The greatest British prime ministers, such as Lord Salisbury, are those who combine clear vision and administrative ability with a deep instinctive sense not only of the way the nation thinks but also of the way it does things—or does not do them. The less great lack the vision, but retain the other qualities. The still less great lack both vision and administrative skill but still possess that indispensable sense of the British attitude. It is a sense that can only spring from sympathy. To be sympathetic towards a point of view or an attitude does not necessarily signify approval. And, in fact, nobody could have disapproved more of the British spirit of muddling through than Lord Salisbury, a great part of whose career was spent on the one hand in a self-sacrificial struggle against its exploitation by a supreme and highly un-English opportunist, Disraeli, and on the other in a battle-royal with the man who embodied it to the point of almost total inertia—his connection, Lord Derby. But although Salisbury fought very hard against the current of the national temperament and devoted his life to trying to make his colleagues think clearly and devise for themselves an active policy, he was at the same time deeply and instinctively aware that, working against the stream, one man however gifted could do nothing. So he rode it. From being a rebel in youth, he became a patient manipulator, in his supreme self-confidence feeling himself under no obligation to point out what he was doing for all to see or to convince or educate those whose stupidities and timidities he despised.

Milner lacked that profound and indestructible self-confidence, or the lazy and dispassionate contempt for fools—or those who differed from him—which is the mark of the English genius. So instead of manipulating he fought. He chafed. He beat his head against a wall, the strongest wall in the history of the world; the wall of invincible self-delusion with which the English surround themselves and their affairs. In this sense, he was a revolutionary: he thought that the leopard might change its spots. He thought that by taking thought and making a mental effort the English might be brought to dominate their fate. In this, of course, he was correct. What he failed always to see was that to ask them to take thought and make a mental effort was asking the impossible.

We may indeed ask whether, had he realised this, he would have committed himself to his policy of bringing the Transvaal quarrel to a head. We have seen with what conscientious pains, brilliant lucidity and swift grasp of essentials he kept in the forefront of all his arguments the necessity of clearing up that pernicious and cancerous situation once and for all and bringing to an end the dilatory hesitations which had for twelve years made the proper development of South Africa an impossibility. He wished to do this by peaceful means; but if peaceful means failed he never shrank from the prospect of war.

Such an attitude implies the belief that firm, decided and consistent action may achieve definite results. This is an irreproachable belief. But what Milner evidently failed to see was that although the English may on occasion bring themselves to firm and decisive action, if invariably too late and without adequate preparation, to ask them for consistent action is too much. In other words, sooner or later, and after the fiercest and most determined effort, the English will always give away what they have won, not as a conscious gesture of abnegation (though they are magnificently capable of this too, and so was Milner), but without in the least realising what they are doing and in a sort of placid drift of mental inertia. Would Milner, in a word, have been so keen for a show-down with the South African Republic had he known that before ten years were out His Majesty's Government would have undone all his work and discarded the fruits of so much sacrifice by so many devoted men? And would he not, had he been the supreme leader which all his gifts seemed to predicate, in fact have known that, the English being what they are, some such final outcome was inevitable? What, then, would his policy have been? He had performed one miracle, which had been made possible, as he knew, by the accident which put the one Englishman under Salisbury capable of conceiving a policy and sustaining it at the Colonial Office. Without Chamberlain he could have done nothing. His whole policy depended on Chamberlain's existence. The policy only made sense if there was a real chance of its being carried through to its logical conclusion, for which the war was hardly more than a clearing of the ground. Yet there was only one Chamberlain, who could not last for ever; and sooner or later the Liberals were bound to come in.

All this is a gross over-simplification of a complex of extreme subtlety. It is made for the sole purpose of showing up Milner's only weakness, his only blind spot, his revolutionary optimism— a strange quality to find in a man popularly notorious as a rigid, cold, aloof reactionary. Furthermore, it is seen only as a weakness in relation to a particular kind of task, the task of the national leader who, provided he understands, to the point of feeling it in his bones, the national temper as it manifests itself in the problems of government, may make a success of the highest office in the land without possessing a tenth of the character and mental equipment with which Milner was endowed—may make a success, that is to say, of holding country and government to-gether. In every other capacity, the qualities of a Milner, including what has just been called his weakness, are of a value inestimable to us though, almost invariably, a curse to their possessors.

In the year of Milner's death, Mr. Stanley Baldwin, then him-self Prime Minister, made a speech at Oxford in which he drama-tised Milner's sense of duty and held him up as a model to all public men. He was referring specifically to Milner's refusal of the Colonial Office when, in 1903, with the war behind him, recon-struction under way, the worst reefs still in the offing, and his reputation at its zenith, he declined Balfour's almost imperative invitation to join the Cabinet.

Let me tell you [Mr. Baldwin said] one story of Lord Milner, which, I expect, will be new to most of you. I tell it to you, not only to show you, if you have any doubt, what manner of man he was, but to show you what the finest type of Englishman at his best can be; the type that all of us would wish to emulate. Twenty-two years ago Lord Milner had completed about two years of work in the restoration of South Africa, one of the most difficult tasks to which any man had ever been called upon to devote himself, and, by confession on all hands, he had accomplished a work which it is doubtful if anyone else could have accomplished. His praise was in all men's mouths. He was a man who loved his own home in his own country, never so happy as when in England, and there came to him at that moment an offer from Lord Balfour to come home as Secretary of State for the Colonies, a task for which he was peculiarly fitted, and in every way he would have delighted in the work. He declined—and why? He declined because he knew that, in spite of the success he had achieved, there were coming years of the utmost difficulty in South Africa, years in which probably he would lose all the popularity he had won, years in which possibly his success might be turned into failure, and he said, 'No, no, I am not going to go away from here and take the credit of accomplishments up to this point, and leave someone else to come out now to face what must be years of difficulty and distress. I am going to see them through myself.'

This shows the finest temper, the finest spirit in which an Englishman could possibly do and face his work.

Few things could show up more sharply the chasm between Milner and the ordinary run of successful English politicians than those orotund phrases which only vulgarise the resolution which they were intended to celebrate and travesty the crisp and unassuming words of the actual refusal:

On September 20th, 1903, he wrote to Mr. Balfour:

. . . I feel much honoured and touched by your kind letter of the 17th. That you should think me worthy of attempting to succeed the greatest Colonial Secretary our country has ever had, is the highest compliment which has ever been paid, or is ever likely to be paid me. It is not, however, any sense of the enormous difficulty of the task, which prevents my accepting your offer, though it would certainly cause me to accept it with diffidence. Neither is it any want of sympathy with your government. Most earnestly do I desire its continuance and success, alike on public and personal grounds. But I am honestly convinced that, at the present juncture, I can render the government and the country better service in the position I actually hold than in the higher office which you offer me. On grounds of health and for other personal reasons I have for some time been anxious to leave South Africa and to enjoy, for a time at any rate, a complete respite from public cares. Mr. Chamberlain has for some time been aware of this wish on my part, but, when he was in South Africa, he impressed upon me most strongly the duty of remaining at my post until the settlement of the new Colonies was more advanced. The arguments which he then urged and to which I yielded, to the extent of promising to return for at least a year after my present holiday, have lost, in my opinion, none of their cogency in the interval. It is true that I should still be dealing with South African affairs at the Colonial Office, but I think that, in a situation which, though improving, is still full of difficulty, my personal influence on the spot has a somewhat special value, and that what the Government might lose by its withdrawal would not be compensated by my bringing a somewhat weary mind to bear on a number of new questions, of which I have no previous experience. A year or eighteen months hence I hope I may retire from South Africa with a good conscience. At present I should retire with an uneasy feeling that I was leaving things at a loose end, and not giving quite a fair chance to my successor. I believe that if I were to go fully into details, you would concur in this view. But it would be unjustifiable to trouble you, especially at a time of such pressure, with a long disquisition. Suffice it to say that, after giving the matter my most earnest consideration, I feel it my duty to stick to the new Colonies as long as, in my judgment, they need me, always provided that I retain the full confidence of H.M. Government, of which, while you are at the head of it, I venture to feel assured. . . .

Thus, in a sense far deeper than Mr. Baldwin's eulogy reveals, everything said in it was true. Milner did deliberately sacrifice himself to duty. He wanted to come home, not to watch wagtails or scratch the backs of pedigree pigs, but because he was ill and tired and stale and needed a rest. But the great sacrifice of refusing office was for him no sacrifice at all, a thing no professional politician is likely to understand.

More importantly, he was already reaching the conclusion that the political game was not for him. A few months after the great refusal he was writing to his intimate friend, Sir Clinton Dawkins, in terms which reveal very clearly his real and private state of mind:

> . . . What has been steadily growing in my mind for years, has now attained the force of a conviction and a resolution. And that is, *tout bonnement*, I will not go on with political life in the ordinary sense of the word, when I am freed from this dungeon. I WILL NOT. What I may do is quite uncertain and I decline, until I have had my long holiday, even to consider it. But I am too far, too increasingly as the years go on, out of sympathy with our political system, and with the political attitude of the bulk of my countrymen, to be a successful politician in the ordinary sense. I am an anachronism. It may be I was born too late, it may be I was born too soon. In the latter, I think the less probable case, I may be of some use in politics —as an outsider, though never again as an active participant in the fray. But I am not going to make myself miserable any more, or to embarrass any Ministry or party, by holding office on the terms, on which under the conditions of our day it can alone be held. Every man can afford to hold *some* unpopular ideas. But I have amassed *all the most unpopular*. I hold, with real conviction, a whole posse of them, and I mean to allow myself the luxury of holding, perhaps even of occasionally expressing them. . . .

He had not started off in that spirit, as we know; nor, as Mr. Baldwin suggested, did he in the least share the professed reluctance for public life fashionable among latter-day politicians. Nor did he love his own home in England above all other things (until, indeed, he gave up South Africa, he did not possess a home: only his old chambers). He had deliberately made a choice, as a poor man with his way to make in the world, between domesticity and a full-dress career—or, rather, his temperament made the choice for him, and he accepted it with open eyes and no illusions. He was also strongly attracted to service abroad. On his return from Egypt he had written to the same friend to whom he now confided his determination to have nothing more to do with a political career, Sir Clinton Dawkins: 'the sober joys of a well-rendered estimate are tame compared with Empire-Making. . . .' And earlier still, to his first chief, Lord Goschen: 'Most men have roots in England, which make them prefer a far lower salary at home. But this is not my case . . . and I shall feel "at home" wherever I am serving, directly or indirectly, the interests of Great Britain. . . .'

This is better than the commonplace image of a man who sacrificed the sweets of office on the one hand and a tweed-clad, pipe-smoking bucolic existence on the other in order not to let the side down. It is better because it is truer. We cannot begin to understand the mind of a Milner unless it is firmly grasped that he was consumed with a sense of vocation: the vocation was the service of his country.

With the sense of vocation, as with missionaries of every kind, goes the danger of fanaticism. This is now so well understood, and the evils of fanaticism have been experienced so sharply in our lives, that the man who believes in an idea is nowadays suspect. Not the least rewarding aspect of the study of Milner's thought and actions is the object-lesson they provide of how high principle, rigorously pursued, can, when combined with high thinking, disassociate itself entirely from fanaticism, which is then seen to have no intrinsic connection with ideas, but only with stupidity or the failure to assimilate ideas.

What, then, lay behind the outburst to Sir Clinton Dawkins? Certainly not, as might at first sight appear to those who do not know Milner well, any bitterness of feeling produced in him by the personal attacks which were then clouding his life. The worst had happened and he was in the pillory. But it is clear from what we have already seen of Milner that he was not a man to turn sour and sulk in face of unjust treatment. And, as we have seen, when the storm came in all its fury and he was subjected to the worst humiliation that can befall a public servant, a formal vote of censure in the House of Commons, he amazed and bewildered all those who did not understand him, and amazed and inspired all those who did, by the extreme and unparalleled generosity of his attitude towards those who had contributed to his tragedy. More than this, when his oldest and bitterest enemy, Lloyd George, called him from retirement to be one of the five Ministers who were given supreme command in 1916, he accepted at once, without a trace of rancour, and set himself to work in unreserved amity with the man who had done more than any other to divide the country against his South African policy. It may be said that his influence on final victory was second only to that of the Prime Minister. There was a job to be done, and he knew he could do it. That, as always, was his only consideration.

A job to be done and the ability to do it. In this phrase is the key to the whole situation. He saw government not as an end in itself, but as the means to a series of ends, correlated to form a policy. He saw himself in South Africa, not as a man chosen to muddle the machine along, steering clear of disaster, but as the chief-of-staff of an operation which was to ensure the best possible deployment of South Africa's resources in the interests of its inhabitants, Great Britain, and the world at large. It was a specific task, and he set about it as such. Chamberlain and Lord Selborne shared his views. But the Government, the Opposition, and the public as a whole did not. The High Commissioner for them, if they ever thought about it seriously, was the man detailed to act as a buffer between themselves and trouble emanating from South Africa—and, into the bargain, to arrange that there should be as little trouble as might be.

Milner learnt this lesson slowly. To the end he does not seem to have realised that he was up against the British version of original sin: inertia, woolly thinking, and self-deception, which, allied with a strong but all too erratic and spasmodically operating social conscience, enters into a truly formidable combination known to foreigners as hypocrisy. To the end he seemed to believe that if only, somehow, you could change the institutions —the System, he called them—you could change the men, forgetting that the System was the proud creation of the men themselves. Long before his outburst to Sir Clinton Dawkins, and while his reputation was still at its zenith, we find him writing

... But the system is wrong.... I set sail in a rotten ship. By the help of the High Gods I may get her into port somehow. Clearly it is my duty to do all I can to that end, not to leave her (unless the rudder is taken out of my hands) till she is in port. But I am under no obligation to take another voyage in her. The day might come—who knows?—when I should have the opportunity of pointing out, *why* we make such a mess of things, and make the burden on the true-hearted servants of the country so unnecessarily heavy; *where* the system is wrong. But I should not attempt that for a long time, not until I could see my own experiences at a true perspective, till personal bitterness had died out of me, as it readily does, with rest and time, and I could speak of it all coolly, with balance, with calm and therefore carrying a conviction, which I could not carry while still heated from the fray and when people might think that anger, disappointment or some personal interest clouded my judgment. From a calm distance, as a man out of the fray for ever, with nothing to gain or lose, I think I might, if I lived and things so shaped themselves, make my *experience* of use to future labourers.

And again, to the same correspondent just a month later:

. . . The worst of it all is, I feel increasingly: *For what* is this sacrifice of life? We have got as good raw material of statesmen as any country ever had. But the system is hopeless. Only one man in a hundred dares give effect or utterance to the statesmanship that is in him, and he, being a solitary incident, is of little use. He may, like Cromer, develop one limb of the body, but of a body paralysed at the centre. It is no use abusing the Ministry. The Ministry has weak members, but it has also very strong ones. As a whole they are a failure. So will their successors be, because there is no consistent national mind about any political question, no *standard*, no cohesion, system, training anywhere. Even the few people who think consistently or constantly about public affairs, and think of them as a whole, such as Leo [Maxse], Spenser Wilkinson, Amery, your humble servant, are all 'on their own' without touch, without being a school, without co-related effort towards common agreed ends, and if we were all in touch we should avail nothing. Perhaps a great *Charlatan*—political scallywag, buffoon, liar, stump orator and in other respects popular favourite—may some day arise, who is nevertheless a *statesman*—the combination is not impossible—and who, having attained and maintaining power by popular art, may use it for national ends. It is an off chance, but I don't see any other. I don't deceive myself. If I am making sacrifices, it is not for this effete and dislocated Body Politic. The Almighty, if he wishes to preserve it, will do so, not assuredly from within, but from without, i.e. by smiting all its competitors (as some of them are already smitten) with similar fatuity. . . .

And finally, three weeks later:

. . . That is what I say 1000 times and shall die saying. *It is not the fault of the men.* Lansdowne is a *good average* man. Joe is an extraordinary man—quite absolutely on the big lines. Under a different system he really might federate the Empire effectively and live in history with the Richelieus. He has most comical weaknesses—look at his impressionability! The most ridiculous incidents—and people —temporarily affect him, and may cause him to make great mistakes. But the effect is only temporary. In the long run he is swayed by big permanent ideas, and they are not external to him, but, wherever he got them from, *they have roots inside him* which alone can insure any vitality to a policy or any greatness to its possessor. Still, even Joe can make nothing great with this *system*, and what do you expect of lesser men?

. . . The effect of the revolt of the better members of a party against the worse hardly ever is to improve the party. It only results in weakening it as a whole and in bringing in the other side. . . .

You may say what *is* the *system* you are always abusing? Well, it is not easy to analyse, all in a hurry, but here are some of its defects.

(1) Ultimate power on all matters, without appeal, with an *ignorant* people, not only ignorant but having no adequate appreciation of the supreme value of trained knowledge, or of the difference in *size* of the questions submitted to them, so that they are capable of the same levity with regard to the biggest things as with regard to trifles.

(2) This disregard, or rather inadequate regard, for trained knowledge and complete information running through the whole people, not merely the groundlings, and finding its expression in the habit of mind and judgment of the upper class and the whole structure of our administration.

(3) Party Politics at their worst, i.e. the old divisions of parties no longer corresponding to any real differences, and representing the mere husks of dead controversies—hence a pure struggle of ins and outs without any inner meaning, or principle in it whatever.

(4) A huge, unwieldy Cabinet, in which half a dozen men of Cabinet rank are swamped by twice the number of second-rate men, who are mere ballast. At ordinary times this does not matter, but in

a storm, shifting ballast may sink a ship. The inert stupid mass wobbles over in a crisis, and you have a disaster. Or, rather, to use your simile, the ruck of the mules stampede, and carry the stronger animals with them, or trample on them in their wild flight.

(5) Above and Before All. No grading of the 100,000 questions, no separating of the local and Imperial, the great and the small, but all ultimately centring in that same unwieldy Cabinet, which, muddling a pension or a 'row in the Guards', may be shaken in its dealings with a national question of the first moment, and in any case cannot give *continuous thought and study* to the *vital*, being eternally distracted by the local and *temporary*, even when not by the absolutely *petty and parish pump*, order of questions. This side of the muddle needs a small volume to develop. . . .

Those six points, looked at coolly, are a strange and illuminating mixture. The first is an outcry against the excesses of democracy, as such. The second has nothing to do with any system, but is a condemnation of one aspect of the British character, manifesting itself at its worst, and most frequently, in a frivolous disregard for facts, but, much more rarely, and at its best, in the fine independence of mind exhibited by her greatest statesmen. It is only in the remaining four points that we come to criticism of the system proper; and on these Milner was to take his stand and fight for the rest of his life, in and out of office— above all the intrusion of party politics into Imperial and foreign affairs. He was the first clear-headed advocate of what the Americans have come to call a bi-partisan policy in dealing with great national problems.

There emerges, thus, the figure of a man who felt too strongly to be satisfied with the instrument at hand. The strength and intensity of his feelings, the passion behind his interventions, however superficially restrained, is manifested over and over again in his letters, his despatches, his speeches. We remember the enthusiasms of his youth; the single-minded ardour with which he threw himself into one test after another: to excel at the University, to reform with Toynbee, to get to the bottom of Karl Marx, of whom nobody had ever heard, to modernise journalism with Stead, to forward the career of his first political chief; we remember the sudden, intense black-out of despair which caused him to tear up his papers for the Ireland scholarship, when it was already won. We remember also his immediate recovery from this black moment ('If you know what it is to be very disappointed without being at all disheartened you know my present state of mind'); and we see it all over again after the failure of the Bloemfontein Conference: 'And so it was a failure—as I anticipated. . . . I am fearfully tired and disappointed, but *not beaten.*' And remembering all this we get some idea of the quickness of feeling behind that cool front and see in his portrait not 'the alert and deadly serious official with close-shut mouth . . . and shrewd eyes looking a little sideways through narrowed lids, weighing up the situation, sizing up his man'—not that, but the iron guard of a man who felt too strongly. He himself knew, as well he might. 'Life has always been an intense thing with me', he wrote from Cape Town to Lady Edward Cecil in the first year of the war, '—despite a certain external quiet, which is well . . . intense in its interests, its affections. I do not wish it otherwise. In the worst moments I say to myself, "If you were not capable of being so wretched, you would not have been capable of being so happy. Is it not worth while? . . . and in the meantime I must make the pain into character. I think one does grow by suffering, if it is not too constant, so as to weaken the love of life."'

It was not because he was too rigid and cold that Milner could never become a national leader. It was because he was not cold enough.

Chapter Sixteen

THE IMPERIAL IDEA

IN THE BEWILDERMENT which so many people feel today we hear increasingly the call for an idea. It is usually called a constructive idea. Only if we can oppose a constructive idea to Communism can we hope to hold our own. And so various bright spirits hand us out a whole series of constructive ideas: Moral Rearmament, Fascism, the Welfare State, European Union. These are all magnificently constructive ideas, and their very multiplicity suggests that it is not for lack of ideas, constructive or otherwise, that we find ourselves today at a loss. At the root of the trouble, of course, is confusion of purpose. Here and now, in the most disillusioned age in history (or so we like to think of it), we suffer still from the perfectionist hang-over of an earlier and very temporary age when, with the help of God and the wonders of science, but principally the latter, we were going to make a perfect world—not a world fit for heroes to live in, because heroes would not be required in that world, but a world in which everyone got everything for nothing: a government of spivs, by spivs, for spivs, as the Edwardian Utopias might be called. The spivs, of course, were all magnificently built, with fair hair, good complexions, and good teeth. They did not wear fancy overcoats. But these were only details. And so we fret because we have not made that perfect world, arrogating to ourselves, by the clearest of implications, the rank of Almighty—a failed Almighty, to be sure, but no less of a god for that. We know, in fact, that we are not almighty after all, but we still somehow feel that we ought to be, and thus be able to produce a perfect world (and the odd thing is that even those who believe in the reality of God, and who should therefore know better than to aspire to omniscience, suffer from this feeling too). The more decent and devout among the Communists still quiver to the first fine careless rapture of the belief in human omnipotence. They really believe, as we in this country believed in the days of cotton exports, cheap coal and *laissez-faire*, that the problem of the universe has been solved, or would be solved if everyone would only go Communist. Our American cousins have the same illusion, with the difference that for them the panacea is the American Way of Life, or Free Enterprise petrified into a dogma. Without trespassing in the field of metaphysics it is possible to doubt whether both can be right. Sticking firmly to common sense, it is impossible to doubt that both are wrong.

In other words, we have been here before. And yet, flying in the face of all our hardly won experience, experience which, properly used, would put us at an immense advantage over those peoples who are engaged in acquiring it, or the Russian and American equivalents, now we call for a constructive idea which, through us, will save the world, ignoring the fact that as sure as fate Soviet Communism and the American Way of Life will go the way of our own insane material optimism of the nineteenth century, leaving Russia and America—where? . . .

As if, in any case, ideas are things to be manufactured. It is exciting to believe that St. Pancras Station, or the Moscow Underground, or the Rockefeller Centre—all these symbols extended to infinity—are the heralds of the millennium. It is fun while it lasts, that is. And this, when you come to think of it, is all that is normally meant by a constructive faith. But once the novelty has worn off and the world is found to be much the same place as before, to go crying for a new faith *in vacuo* is about as edifying as to sigh for the lost joys of tin soldiers. All we need, and we either have it or we do not, is a belief in ourselves, which, with or without an emphasis on divine authority for it, has been the only force to sustain man for the untold generations of his experience —except for those few, crowded years of aberration when it was replaced by a belief in the machine.

And this, to come round to our subject, is what Milner was really about, and why it seems to me that although some of his examples are out of date, the core of his simple but extremely stalwart thought is as valid today as it was fifty years ago—and a great deal more likely to arouse an intelligent response.

But who are we, who must believe in ourselves?

The *sine qua non* of any coherent society, or family, is a common code of behaviour. The code may be broken as often as not, but it must be firmly believed in by the majority, and by them enforced as completely as may be. Such codes are not elaborated out of the blue: they slowly grow. Governing the world as a whole there is no such code, and attempts by international lawyers to devise one which will be observed have not so far met with success. This is not to say that there may not already exist in the hearts of the majority of at least the leading peoples the rudiments of such a code, and, with the rate the world moves in these days, it may grow and develop a good deal faster than anyone who thought seriously about it would have predicted fifty years ago. For the time being it does not effectively exist, and the nation, or the race, as Milner called it, until now is the largest society in which it does exist. It is the largest society, that is to say, in which the individual may feel completely at home and get on with whatever he wants to do protected on both flanks. This is so and must be. Invocations of the past to prove otherwise are misleading if not false. Thus it is wholly beside the point to draw a parallel between the United Europe which figures so largely in our thoughts today with the so-called united Europe under the authority of Rome—the Popish Rome. Quite apart from the fact that Europe was not then united but was a cockpit of war and oppression, the attempts at unity were not concerned with the peoples: they were no more than unions of the ruling families, which is very different from a union of nation-states. In those days the ruling families of Europe belonged to a larger family which possessed a common code of sorts: they were thus far closer to each other than to the common people over whom, in various languages, they ruled. Whether the end of this arrangement was advantageous to the people as a whole is neither here nor there. It has come to an end. It cannot be repeated. And the popular nation-states which have taken the place of feudal principalities and kingdoms have not yet developed a common code. There are a thousand and one ways in which such a code may be induced to develop, and some of these are being tried. But the best way, as usual, is by example. If we believe in our own code, we, the British, and develop it as best we may, and if it is worth all that we think it is, sooner or later it will catch on—as to quite a surprising extent it has already caught on. If we do not believe in our own code, then certainly we are in no position to add to the common stock of experience, so it would be more public-spirited altogether to throw in our hand and have done with it. If we believe in it and it proves to be worthless, then the world will profit that much from this discovery. In any case, the best contribution we can make to the world as a whole is to go on developing ourselves and our own interests according to our lights and hope that things will come right. Interest is not the same as acquisition. It could conceivably be to our interest to make great material sacrifices of one kind or another. But we should do this, even to the extent of surrendering part of our sovereignty, only because we believed it to be in our own national interest and for no other reason at all. To perform such actions in what is called the interest of humanity at large is a sort of arrogance which will bring its own retribution. Because we know nothing about humanity at large, which adheres to a multiplicity of codes, some of them directly opposed to our own.

Thus Milner could still say, with perfect justice, as he said in 1906 to Mr. Amery's constituents at Wolverhampton, citizens of a much more reasonable world than we inhabit today:

> I am afraid I am not large-minded enough to be interested in the total wealth of the world [he was campaigning for tariff-reform], even if I were sure, which I am not, that universal, unregulated competition was going to produce the greatest total wealth. My ideal is to see the greatest number of people living healthy and independent lives by means of productive work in our own country. ... The conception which haunts me is the conception of the people of these islands as a great family, bound by indissoluble ties to kindred families in other parts of the world, and within its own borders striving after all that makes for productive power, for social harmony, and, as a result of these and as the necessary

complement and shield of these, for its strength as a nation among the nations of the world.

All this means, really, is that it is no good biting off more than you can chew, that the better is the enemy of the good (a favourite phrase of Milner's), that to look after your own and behave as well as you can according to your lights is all that can be asked of man and a good deal more than he is likely to perform, and that the surest way to upset the apple-cart is to abandon what you more or less understand in order to involve yourself in something you don't understand at all—or, supreme human folly, to embark on a large-scale enterprise in the hope of covering the failure of your small one. The Victorians had a word for it, when it came to money, which they understood: 'Look after the pence and the pounds will look after themselves.' That system may or may not work in the days of the atom-bomb: it has yet to be tried. What is quite certain is that no other system will work. It never has.

It is characteristic of Milner that he indulged in no generalisations of this kind. Apart from one or two broad statements on Imperialism, everything he had to say was tacked firmly to some practical issue. This wholly admirable trait went with his lack of demagogy and was largely responsible for the popular failure to understand what he was really after. In order to outline the body of his thought, we are thus forced to work through his speeches and writings on a number of apparently disconnected topics: the British Empire as such; party government; conscription; social reform; sweated labour; free trade and tariff reform; imperial preference; land settlement in South Africa; economic policy; the trade union movement; and so on. This is not only characteristic, it is also extremely revealing: it is a direct reflection of the quality which made his mind all of a piece. He believed, as we have seen, in the survival of Britain and the British race through the Empire. This was his general idea; and everything he said or did followed naturally from that. Thus when he argued about free trade and tariff reform he related these matters to his central belief, the survival of Britain, and to nothing else at all. Tariff reform and imperial preference were necessary for the welfare of the Empire. And when he argued about education or sweated labour, it was the same: the one had to be developed, the other to go, for the health of the Empire. It was the same with everything he touched. And the result was that instead of being disconnected, as, because of our normal habit of mind, these various causes and a multitude of others are liable to seem, they all formed a part of a whole, of, in a word, a coherent *policy*. Thus if Milner had had his way, there would have been no question, as in fact there habitually is, of a Treasury policy, a Board of Trade policy, a housing policy, an education policy, a foreign policy, a colonial policy, all arrived at—if indeed they ever are arrived at—independently, and governed by a thousand different and often conflicting pressures: there would have been one all-embracing British policy directed at the survival of the British Empire in a hostile world, and no other interest at all would have been allowed to interfere with the expression of this policy in every aspect of the administration.

There is a beautiful example of the strength of this attitude in a speech made to the Manchester Conservative Club on December 14th, 1906, at a time when the impassioned interest of the Liberal Government, and above all of Mr. Lloyd George, in social reform as such, as an end in itself, had swept everything else out of their minds.

For what is it that we are told has turned aside the thoughts and affections of men from this dream, this mirage, or, to use an even more opprobrious epithet, this fetish of Imperialism? It is the growth of interest in what is known as social reform. Social reform! I take that to mean the movement, long since potent and no doubt of growing strength, which seeks to employ the resources and energies of the State in ameliorating the condition of the mass of the people, in raising their material, intellectual, moral standard of life, in giving even the humblest cause to rejoice in his birthright as a British citizen. And that, beyond all doubt or question, is a noble ideal. All of us must sympathise with it. I for one, not being and never having been a votary of *laissez-faire*, not only sympathise with it, but believe that the action of the State can do a great deal to promote it. And I would rather see statesmen make many mistakes, as they will make mistakes, in their efforts to attain that end, than shrink from such efforts because of the pitfalls which beset them. Yes. By all means social reform. But where is the antagonism between it and

Imperialism? To my mind they are inseparable ideals, absolutely interdependent and complementary to one another. How are you going to sustain the vast fabric of the Empire? No single class can sustain it. It needs the strength of the whole people. You must have soundness at the core—health, intelligence, industry; and these cannot be general without a fair average standard of material well-being. Poverty, degradation, physical degeneracy—these will always be. But can any patriot, above all any Imperialist, rest content with our present record in these respects? If he cares for the Empire, he must care that the heart of the Empire should beat with a sounder and less feverish pulse.

And then he goes on to give the reverse side of the picture. If social reform is necessary for the well-being of the Empire, so, without the well-being of the Empire, there can be no lasting social reform:

But, on the other hand, what is going to become of all your social well-being if the material prosperity which is essential to it, though not identical with it, is undermined? And you cannot have prosperity without power, you, of all peoples, dependent for your very life, not on the products of these islands alone, but on a world-wide enterprise and commerce. This country must remain a great Power or she will become a poor country; and those who in seeking, as they are most right to seek, social improvement are tempted to neglect national strength, are simply building their house upon sand. . . . These islands by themselves cannot always remain a Power of the very first rank. But Greater Britain may remain such a power, humanly speaking, for ever, and by so remaining, will ensure the safety and prosperity of all the states composing it, which, again humanly speaking, nothing else can equally ensure. That surely is an object which in its magnitude, in its direct importance to the welfare of many generations, millions upon millions of human beings, is out of all proportion to the ordinary objects of political endeavour.

If this is not a constructive idea, it is hard to see what is. A constructive idea is essentially a unifying purpose. No purpose can unify unless it can come naturally to a great number of people and, at the same time, promise at least some measure of attainment. It can promise no measure of attainment unless all those believing in it know instinctively how to work together and can hope to achieve a practical level of agreement as to the best means of achieving it. The peace of the world organised on a global scale and from a common neutral centre is undoubtedly a purpose which comes naturally to a great many people, but it promises no measure of attainment for the simple reason that all those believing in it do not know instinctively how to work together and cannot hope to achieve a practical level of agreement as to the best means of achieving it. Furthermore, many of the millions believing in it have no control of their own destinies, but, on the contrary, are subject to the rule of others who do not believe in it. The peace of the world, centrally organised, thus does not qualify as a constructive idea or a unifying purpose. The highest unifying purpose on the secular level so far available to men is patriotism. The highest form of patriotism so far available to the British people is Imperial patriotism. This, if steadfastly pursued at the time when Milner was preaching it, might have saved the world from two great wars. In discarding it as an unworthy idea in favour of two attempts to organise world peace directly, first through free trade, then through the League of Nations, we threw away the substance for the shadow.

Chapter Seventeen

PARTIES AND EMPIRE

IT WAS THE substance that Milner wanted. His life was a fight for it. His refusal to take office may now be seen as an admission of defeat on one front; but he continued the battle on another. That is to say, he saw quite clearly as far back as the year 1902 not only that he could not hope to win that battle, or even fight it single-mindedly, inside the Government machine, but also that the acceptance of office would place him in a false position, since it would mean his tacit acceptance of a system which he rejected.

The truth is [he writes in the preface to *The Nation and Empire*], as it seems to me, that there is no object of supreme national importance at the present time, which can be attained by the method of party conflict. Imperial Union certainly cannot be, but no more can a sound system of National Defence, or the solution of the Irish Problem, or the repair of the mutilated constitution of the United Kingdom. . . . And if this is the case in the purely political field, it is surely no less true of the economic and social problems, of which all thoughtful men recognise the urgency. In none of these directions is there much to hope from the competition of rival bands of politicians in devising superficially attractive panaceas.

This may be an entirely mistaken view, but it is one which has grown upon me in the course of a well-meant effort not to appear too singular, but to work for the causes, which I believe in, without departing altogether from the conventional lines of party controversy. It is not pleasant to have, after all, to confess oneself an eccentric, still less to run the risk of being derided as a 'superior person'. So far from being justly regarded in that light, I am very conscious of my own inferiority—certainly in effectiveness—to the ardent and whole-hearted party man. But then his chief strength lies in the conviction that the victory of his party means the salvation of the State. If all the objects one most cares about are hopeless unless they become national, if they seem utterly unattainable by the means of a mere party victory, it is difficult to throw oneself into the party fight with the necessary enthusiasm. Of course there is always the danger that, if you don't preach from a party platform, you won't get anybody to listen to you at all. But one has to take some risks in this world. And on the whole I am inclined to think that there is a sufficiently widespread and increasing weariness of the partisan treatment of every great national question to give the exponents of a different method a chance.

When it came to Imperial affairs he was far more explicit, and the case he made for their isolation from party politics was, once the premises were accepted, unanswerable. Unfortunately it could never be argued out to a finish because the premises themselves were not accepted, the premises outlined in the last chapter, that is to say, that the survival of Britain through the preservation and development of the Empire was the supreme concern of all Englishmen. So that the premises themselves became, in a sense, a party issue, although, in fact, few of the Liberals and Socialists who regarded the Empire with suspicion would have been prepared to liquidate it, boldly. Therein lay the disastrous illogicality of their attitude. They blew neither hot nor cold, and they frittered away all chance of Imperial union on a grand scale not out of deep and passionate conviction but to win elections with the aid of a farthing off the loaf.

We have already seen the party spirit in action as applied to South Africa, above all in the stillborn Lyttelton Constitution and in the matter of Chinese labour. But Milner went deeper than those specific questions. He was criticising the system long before he publicly suffered at its hands. A great deal of our unpreparedness for the Boer War is directly attributable to the party spirit bearing down upon Joseph Chamberlain, who, of all men, struggled manfully to ignore it. It was the same party spirit which was later to drive Mr. Baldwin on his own astonishing confession to conceal from the country the need for rearmament, because he knew that the call to arms would lose him an election. Not, and here is the crux, because the people of the country would not have responded to a reasoned plea, but because the Opposition would have made a reasoned plea impossible and would have appealed to the less reputable instincts of the people for the sake of regaining power. It is the same party spirit which prevents at this moment of writing, and has for the past five years prevented, His Majesty's Government on the one hand, and on the other His Majesty's Opposition from telling the people the hard facts about our battle for survival and recommending the necessarily unpleasant measures required to meet it—with the result that we have allowed ourselves to slide into increasing dependence on America.

All this suggests that the trouble is not the party spirit as such, which may once have fulfilled a most useful function, but the impact of the party spirit on a mass democracy. In the days when the franchise was limited and the country governed by a small caste of hereditary rulers and administrators, the party system was at least a useful check on the abuse of power. But when the sovereign people, the masses, came to hold the power of life and death over every government, this particular check was no longer necessary, and the Opposition programme, no longer a dagger at the throat of overweening Governmental presumption, became an instrument for bamboozling the mass electorate into voting it into office.

Milner made no attempt to condemn party government lock, stock, and barrel. He simply wanted it kept out of the larger national questions. And since he himself was above all interested in the larger national questions, he had little personal use for it:

> Do not let me be thought to suggest that Imperial affairs are necessarily of greater dignity and importance than local affairs, or that a man is better employed in concerning himself with the former rather than with the latter. . . . The point is, that Imperial and local affairs are different in character, and that the same men are not generally, or often, equally well qualified, by inclination and experience, to deal with both. A system which makes successful activity in the one sphere the only avenue to influence in the other, involves enormous waste.

He then goes on to state categorically and for the public ear what he has so often said in private:

And that is not the only, or the greatest evil arising from the present subordination of Imperial to local politics. Its worst consequence is that it carries the corroding influence of party spirit into a region in which existing party divisions are wholly out of place. Those divisions owe their origin to conflicts of opinion about domestic questions. It is true that they have a tendency, even in the field of their origin, to outlive the differences of principle from which they sprang, and that the party fight thus becomes a mere scramble for power. It is true that in that scramble men are constantly compelled to sacrifice their convictions to the imperious call of party discipline. But with regard to domestic questions, or at least some of them, party distinctions still have some vestige of meaning. With regard to almost any Imperial question they have absolutely none. And yet no sooner does any Imperial problem assume a character of real urgency, no sooner does it pass out of the region of theoretical discussion into that of practical politics, than it is almost certain to become the shuttlecock of party. For the Government of the day is then obliged to take some line about it. That line may be determined by all sorts of considerations having very little to do with the matter itself. But whatever line the Government takes, the leaders of the Opposition will be tempted to cast about for a different line, and it is ten to one that they will be successful in their quest. And the rank and file on either side will feel in duty bound to follow, though it is out of all reason to suppose that if left to form a genuine opinion— on an entirely new subject—they would find themselves arrayed in two conflicting groups, precisely coinciding with two normal parties. And this edifying process is likely to be going on simultaneously in every part of the Empire, which enjoys the blessing of Parliamentary government, with regard to every new question of urgency that affects them at all.

He did not dwell on his South African experience, as he might in all fairness have done. Bygones were bygones. Or, in his own words: '. . . in a sense I do acquiesce. I bow to fate. Nothing is more repugnant to me than to go on bewailing evils which I am powerless to exorcise.' The South African settlement could not be undone; and no man worked more loyally than Milner to make the best of a bad job. But there were other issues which were by no means finally settled, above all the issue of Imperial Preference, and on these he fought long and hard. Imperial Preference, in

particular, he took as the classic example of the wanton and in-
sensate ruination of an all-important issue by party manœuvring.

In Africa he could take no part in the political campaign for
Tariff Reform initiated by Joseph Chamberlain in 1902 after his
return from Cape Town. But the cause of binding the Empire
closer together by means of preferential tariffs was immediately
his own, and as soon as he was released from all official ties he
made his voice heard. For him, as for Chamberlain, the campaign
for Imperial Preference, which killed Chamberlain's own political
career and more than any other single factor led to the Liberal
landslide in 1906, was nothing less than a crusade. It was the
practical and concrete expression of his whole Imperial credo.

'Whatever the merits or defects of that proposal, its object was
undoubtedly laudable', he was to write in *The Nation and Empire*,
in that vein of grey understatement, so different from the style of
his letters and despatches, or that of his fighting speeches, into
which he fell when trying to confine in measured prose the
deepest passions of his mind.

> It was prompted by motives of Imperial patriotism. By no
> possibility could it serve any partisan purpose, indeed its author
> must have been well aware of the risk which it involved to his party,
> and to his own position as a party leader. Perhaps he hoped that in
> breaking entirely fresh ground he would open a new era in our
> political life, and that, if he failed to convince some of his own
> associates, he would, on the broad Imperial issue, gain the support
> of the mass of his fellow-countrymen, irrespective of party. But
> the sequel was destined to show the impossibility, under present
> conditions, of keeping party considerations from exercising a
> decisive influence upon the fate of any political movement however
> novel, however remote from current topics of party controversy.

In other words the whole tremendous and visionary idea was
killed at birth by the cry of 'a farthing on the loaf . . .'

> It was a chance of a lifetime. And so the broad and far-reaching
> question of principle, which Mr. Chamberlain had raised, was hardly
> discussed. The reasons, and they were grave reasons, which had
> led him to risk everything for the adoption of Imperial Preference,
> were treated as of no account. All the rhetorical batteries of the

Opposition were concentrated upon those details of his scheme which lent themselves to the creation of unreasoning prejudice and exaggerated alarm. A duty which might, or might not, have added a farthing to the price of the quartern loaf, was represented as threatening millions of people with famine. The idea, that closer commercial relations between the different parts of the Empire were of value in promoting amity and co-operation in other respects, was denounced as reliance on 'sordid bonds'. . . . All that happened in this case was bound to happen, the moment the new issue raised by Mr. Chamberlain was sucked into the vortex of our local party struggle. . . . And the consequence is that the people of Great Britain have never yet had a fair chance of looking at the policy of Preference in an atmosphere unclouded by the dust of the party scrimmage.

The solution, to him, was self-evident: an Imperial Constitution.

Essentially what is wanted is discrimination—the separation of Imperial from local interests in the sphere of politics and administration. . . . But for that end we require an Imperial Constitution, providing for the separation of those branches of public business which, like Foreign Affairs, Defence and Ocean Communications, are essentially Imperial, from those which are mainly or wholly local, and for the management of the former by a new authority, representative of all parts of the Empire, but undistracted by the work and the controversies which are peculiar to any single part. We have already, in the United Kingdom, differentiated downwards, by relegating to new organs of government, such as Borough and County Councils, a great many duties formerly performed, or not performed, by the central Government. And the effect has undoubtedly been salutary. We have yet to differentiate upwards, throughout the Empire by entrusting to a body constituted *ad hoc* the matters of common interest, which are at present partially and spasmodically managed, or wholly neglected, by the so-called 'Imperial' Parliament and the Government dependent on it, and to some, though to a much smaller extent, by the Parliaments and Governments of the Dominions. When that day comes, it does not indeed follow that Imperial affairs will be wisely conducted. But they will certainly stand a better chance than they do at present.

Milner did not get his Imperial Constitution. The Empire is not what it was when he wrote that appeal in 1913. In a sense it is stronger: two wars have bound us together, and the Ottawa Conference between the wars established the principle of Imperial Preference, though all too precariously. But all those 'elements tending to disruption' which he saw at the beginning of the century flourish and multiply. Largely through our own fault, the great new nation states which then wanted to draw closer have become more conscious of their separate destinies and find these destinies, moreover, especially in the case of Canada, more closely bound up with other powers than Britain than seemed likely even thirty years ago. The race with time which Milner spoke of in 1913 might appear to have been lost. The fierce pressure against Imperial Union which then came from the Liberal Party has been taken over by the United States of America, which for deep and complicated reasons has never been able to believe in the reality of the Empire, much less in its desirability. The Empire nevertheless continues, though under another name; and although the end envisaged by Milner may never be reached —can, in an exact sense, never now be reached—a good deal still remains materially, and spiritually our awareness of the part it may still be has grown immensely and is still growing. It is something like a revolution to find the Labour Party of Great Britain becoming Imperially minded. If it is not too late; if, that is to say, the Empire is no longer to be frittered away but is to enter on a new lease of life and fulfil its still vast potentialities, our debt to the man who above all others held to the idea will be beyond all measuring.

Shortly before he died, in the last essay in *Questions of the Hour*, he repeated his faith:

Thus there is already in existence, in practical operation over a great part of the world, an agency to promote those very objects which the all-embracing League of Nations, as yet in the far distance, is intended to secure. The British Empire, keeping the peace within its own borders, bound in its own interests, by the very nature of its constitution, to 'seek peace and ensue it' everywhere, is the most powerful bulwark in the world today against the spread of international discord. The maintenance of the strength, the preservation of the unity of that Empire is not the only contribution, but it is by far the greatest and most practical contribution, which British statesmanship can make to the welfare of mankind.

If those words today, uttered with the freshness of a fighting truth in 1922, have a somewhat hollow sound, we have to ask ourselves who made them hollow.

Chapter Eighteen

THE SINS OF FREE ENTERPRISE

'THERE IS NO pain like the pain of a new idea.' This was one of Milner's favourite sayings. And he was always providing new ideas. Or, rather, within the framework of his great conception, old ideas became new and were given active meaning. Thus social reform in his eyes became a burning practical issue, inextricably linked up with the imperative needs of the country and the Empire—with national service, with an emigration policy, with education, with agriculture. And with this capacity to turn static or academic or sentimental ideas into dynamic ideas, went his freedom of mind, upon which we have already commented, the power to see the reality behind the convention, the power of the artist, the power of the man who saw through the Emperor's new clothes. And, with this power, the honesty to give expression to what he saw.

'Lancashire is not free trade. Lancashire is cotton export.' Or, and with a topical ring—though these words were written in the panic economy and export drive after the First World War: 'Is there not indeed some danger of our making a fetish of our export trade? It seems at times to be strangely forgotten that the laborious business of importing and exporting is not an end in itself.' Or, on the subject of conscription, replying to Haldane in 1907:

> If it is the duty, and he says it is the duty, of every able-bodied man, if need be, to defend his country, it cannot be a secondary or subordinate duty. If it is a duty at all, it is a very big duty. Why then object, and worse than object, why denounce and hold up your hands in horror at the idea of that duty being enforced by law, as every other civic duty, including many minor ones, is enforced? You do not leave it optional to a man to pay his taxes.

We cannot follow Milner through all the ideas for which he fought. They may be found in his three books: *England in Egypt, The Nation and the Empire,* and *Questions of the Hour,* just as the whole South African story is unfolded in meticulous and fascinating detail by Mr. Headlam in his two great volumes of the Milner papers. Sooner or later another hand will perform the same service for Milner's last phase, using the Cabinet papers to reconstruct his activity as member of the War Cabinet, as Secretary for War and Secretary for the Colonies, from 1917 to 1921. What we have been concerned with here is to establish the quality of his mind and to isolate the ruling idea to which all his thought was instinctively related: 'The maintenance of the strength, the preservation of the unity of that Empire is not the only contribution, but it is by far the greatest and most practical contribution, which British statesmanship can make to the welfare of mankind.'

He was not in the least afraid of where this purpose might take him. He picked up his ideas where he found them, and made them his own. They came from wide reading as well as from the deepest recesses of his own creative mind. They came from all countries. He lived before the Nazis had been heard of and he died before Moscow Communism had become visible to the world as a coherent system. But, as we have seen, he knew all about Marx in the days when he was simply a stuffy old man living out at Finchley, and brought the same mind to bear on *Das Kapital* that he was later to bring to bear on the reconstruction of South Africa and the problems of industry after the First World War. He rejected Marx, as he rejected Lassalle:

Lassalle and Marx are both men of the highest education, the widest learning and of the most unbounded intellectual pride. . . . Each is equally convinced that he has probed philosophy to the bottom and has the secret of all human history in his pocket. Lassalle probably thought Marx rather a pedant, and Marx certainly thought Lassalle very much an impostor, but Lassalle thought Lassalle and Marx thinks Marx the incarnation of all human wisdom. And without going quite that length, I think every impartial student will be forced to admit of both of them, however unwilling each may be to admit it of the other, that they are both men of immense power.

He rejected their teaching, but to Lassalle's ranging genius and to Marx's now familiar method he felt deeply beholden. And in those early lectures, sixty-eight years ago at Toynbee Hall when he was twenty-eight and on the threshold of his Imperial career, he gave a statement of his own image of human progress which was to remain with him all his life and without a knowledge of which it is impossible to appreciate the real value of his later teaching:

> Let me impress on you [said this man who was to be known to many as the arch-reactionary] once more, in conclusion, that Socialism is nothing novel or monstrous, but something that more or less exists in all human life and society; that it is at present forcing itself forward with unusual energy because in the immediate past it has been unduly discredited, and that its ultimate success depends not upon the premature introduction of a social order for which men are not yet morally fit, but on the gradual growth, if we may hope for such a growth, of individual unselfishness, of a higher sense of the value and the beauty of common work and common enjoyment and of nobler aims than of individual money-getting. Not the subordination of self to community, but a noble ideal of self-development—a self-development that will lead men to seek that kind of wealth in obtaining which they are despoiling no one, which will be to the advantage and not to the detriment of others—is the only durable foundation of a Socialistic State. Only when that ideal has been attained, if it ever is attained, by a predominant number of men, will progress be able to dispense with the present harsh and mean stimulants to personal exertion. In that day Socialism will come about of itself, but before that day every attempt to introduce it as a general system would mean failure, though each state in moral progress will be marked by an increase of Socialism in political institutions. In our present imperfect state, therefore, we can neither afford altogether to follow or altogether to dispense with Socialist ideals; not to follow them altogether because that would be to impose upon mankind a code which they have not yet the wisdom to appreciate or the virtue to observe; not altogether to dispense with them, because that would be to suffer the meaner and more unscrupulous among us to drag us all down to their own level. And as for the violence and exaggeration which attend the first appearance of Socialist doctrine in certain places, do not let them blind you to

the essential truths which animate it. There are violence and exaggeration in the train of every great movement, in the train of Christianity, in the train of the Reformation. It is for us to distinguish the true from the false, to balance carefully and severally the proposals of Socialism, while not forgetting their connection, and to preserve our reverence for what is pure and true and noble in its ideals, while remembering the difficulties which beset their realisation and the danger of attempting to realise them too soon. For here as elsewhere one needs a warm heart and a cool head.

We have seen him wondering whether he was born too soon or too late. Probably too late, he decided. But if proof were needed that in fact he was born too soon those words alone would supply it. They crackle across the gap of half a century like an electric spark between two poles, bringing the past flooding into the present and short-circuiting the great irrelevancy of our time: the Liberal fallacy. For here is the reason why Milner, who had no sympathy with parties, nevertheless became a Conservative. And here is the fundamental, the only real, opposition of our day. Indeed, if we had only seen it as Milner saw it, exploring the new social-consciousness among the working-men of Bermondsey as the nineteenth century swung into decline, here was the fundamental, the only real, opposition of half a century. It is the opposition between those who believe that men are made by institutions and those who believe that institutions are made by men. And since neither statement is the absolute truth, here is a conflict which, conscientiously fought out, should have been most fruitful of creative compromise. But the Liberal fallacy, ignoring the history of millennia, and with it every known fact of life, including the very nature of man himself, obscured this profound opposition for something like half of one of the most critical centuries in the story of the world. It dragged across the wasted years the red-herrings of individual freedom existing in a vacuum and an impossible economic dogma, petrified out of the brief interlude of British industrial monopoly, that the destiny of man should be settled by the principle of buying cheap and selling dear.

It is often said by Liberals today that Conservatism and Labour are closer together than either of them is to Liberalism. Nothing could be more true, and yet the significance of this truth seems to escape those who most clearly state it. For the approximation of Conservatism and Labour is not one of method but of aim: both want a healthy and strong society, but each has a different idea of the best way to achieve it. The good of society, however, comes before the good of the individual. The Liberal, by definition, is not interested in society: he is interested in the freedom of the individual to realise his full potentialities. Only through this, he says, can a healthy society ensue. The Conservative and the Socialist are thus firmly based in reality: the good of society is at least a practical aim the success of which may be measured by pragmatic standards, which may vary from time to time and from society to society. In it individuals may work together, subordinating themselves, more or less, to an agreed and common purpose. But the good of the individual cannot be measured by pragmatic standards, since only the individual, if even he, can tell what it is: it conflicts, moreover, inevitably with the good of other individuals. Thus Liberalism is forced into the curious contradiction that the authority of society as a whole—which even Liberals would not do without—is to be directed to securing for the individual, for countless individuals, their individual good which society has no means of determining and which, if achieved, would multifariously conflict with that very authority which secured it for them. Since it appears to be a fact of life that no individual anywhere can ever achieve the fulfilment of his whole potentiality, the argument for individual self-fulfilment is question-begging and irrelevant, based on a premise for which no authority exists.

They went noiselessly over mats of starry moss, rustled through interspersed tracts of leaves, skirted trunks with spreading roots whose mossed rinds made them like hands wearing green gloves; elbowed old elms and ashes with great forks, in which stood pools of water that overflowed on rainy days, and ran down their stems in green cascades. On older trees still than these huge lobes of fungi grew like lungs. Here, as everywhere, the Unfulfilled Intention, which makes life what it is, was as obvious as it could be among the depraved crowds of a city slum. The leaf was deformed, the curve was crippled, the taper was interrupted; the lichen ate the vigour of the stalk, and the ivy slowly strangled to death the promising sapling.

In that brooding description by Thomas Hardy of the forest home of *The Woodlanders* is a picture of the actual mechanics of the universe based on exact observation. It is also an image of the world in which the individual is free to follow his own bent and develop himself as best he can unrestrained by the coercion of the state. Many descriptions of this world, based on exact observation, may be found in the reports of the Commissions which paved the way for the Factory Acts.

Liberals, of course, even the most doctrinaire, when it comes to domestic matters abandon their own logic. Because a passionate championship of the individual is the mark of a naturally free and ranging spirit, just as the guardianship of the oppressive State is the mark of the ignoble, Liberalism was a product of the humane and idealistic, whose concern for the fate of their fellow-men quite overcame their doctrinal abhorrence of State power, so that, flouting all logic, they put law after law on the Statute Book designed to coerce the strong into caring for the weak. They became, in a word, the 'progressive' party. On the face of it, it might be asked, why all this fuss about doctrine? In practice, whatever they may say about the iniquity of State power they use it, defying jungle law. But the contradiction remains. Their championship of social reform, backed by State intervention, is a tribute to their hearts rather than to their heads. And this contradiction has blurred half a century of political thought. For although in domestic affairs the suffering of the weak, of their fellow-countrymen, overcame and made nonsense of their glorification of the innate right of the individual, in one sphere, in the sphere of international trade, where the consequences of jungle law, owing to a historical accident, were not so immediately apparent, they clung with the tenacity of fanaticism to the idea of total freedom, convincing themselves that in the free market was a natural law of human development which, contrary to all experience and to every other natural law known to mankind, was beneficent in its working.

To buy cheap and to sell dear. The products of sweated labour are cheap. We have stopped sweated labour at home, with the aid of all the coercive authority of the accursed State. But we have not stopped sweated labour in Japan—or Russia. 'Stolen goods', said Milner in 1906, 'are also cheap. Pirated books are cheap. Goods made in violation of a patent are cheap. The setting up of cheapness as the sole and final test is an anarchic principle.'

It also all but lost us an Empire. For, more than anything else, the rejection of the idea of Imperial Preference in favour of the sacred cow of Free Trade contributed to the loosening of those Imperial bonds which Milner gave his life to strengthen. Thus, in coming to Tariff Reform by way of Egdon Heath, we see it in its true perspective, at any rate in the perspective in which Milner saw it, not as a fiscal matter, but as an affair of life and death bearing directly on the future of the British people, and therefore of the world. 'I am not a Tariff Reformer because I am a Conservative; I am a Conservative because I am a Tariff Reformer,' Milner once said. That no longer seems extravagant, and it is hard to think of a better reason for a man of Milner's character for voting with the Party which inevitably attracts along with some of the best many of the worst men in the world—inevitably, because the party intent on the conservation and slow extension of the small island of order and decency in the middle of the universal wilderness, as opposed to the party which risks existing gains for hypothetical benefits to come, will of necessity attract the most interested upholders of the *status quo*, those who have grabbed and held.

Milner, as we have seen, was not interested in parties as such. He was interested even in systems only in so far as they worked or did not work. Today, when half the good ideas in the world are suspect, if not denounced outright, because they have been followed up by Communists on the one hand or Nazis on the other, his cool and candid gaze would have picked out some most striking anomalies in the way we carry on. Nothing could be easier, in fact, than to pick phrases out of the speeches of this great Imperialist to prove that he was at heart a Nazi—or a Communist. Nothing would have affected him less. If he had bothered to argue at all he would have said that so long as it worked the system did not matter in the least. All that mattered was the spirit in which power was exercised. The sort of men who flourish as Nazi or Communist leaders would succeed in degrading any system in the world. The only proof that the Nazi system or the Communist systems are bad is that they will not work and cannot work except in the hands of such men. But that is very far from saying that the whole spirit which brought these systems into being was an evil spirit or that neither contained ingredients which were not admirable in themselves. To attribute a line of thought to a man who is no longer living to repudiate it is always a hazardous thing. But in the light of all we have seen of Milner's mind there can be little doubt that he would have been deeply concerned today by the increasing paralysis of political thought caused by the panic rejection of large series of ideas which happened to have been exploited by evil men operating mistaken systems of government.

He was more radical than the radicals: palliatives were not enough when it came to social reform: '. . . every wise man would rather strike at the causes of low wages and irregular employment than merely mitigate its effects. The necessity of old age pensions is a confession of national failure. It is due, in part at least, to the immense output of unskilled labour—boys and girls thrown upon the world to pick up a few shillings by casual work, without any special training or aptitude for anything.'

He took ideas, was not afraid to take ideas, from militarist Germany: his demand for conscription had its roots in an experience of his youth when, walking with his father in the wake of the advancing German army, he had seen what can happen to a country unprepared and untrained. He was interested in military training, as he was in education, both general and technical, as a means of building up a sturdy and healthy people.

All these things were subordinate to the supreme goal of a strong and enlightened Empire, which depended, he saw, on a constant flow outwards of first-class human material. His belief in State education and then in military service for the country would indeed have done credit to a Nazi—or a Communist. But the end was not a Nazi or a Communist end:

Sooner or later the burden must become too heavy for the un-aided strength of that portion of the race which, at any given time, dwells in the United Kingdom.

For the future growth of that portion is sternly restricted by physical conditions, and it has parted, and must continue to part, with much of its best blood and sinew to build up other lands. The population of these islands cannot greatly increase in numbers with-out declining in quality, and the quality of a large proportion of it ... is already below the standard which we ought to maintain. A better distribution of the people between town and country, and greater attention to physical training, would allow of the healthy development of our present numbers, perhaps of slightly larger numbers. But, with even the best of management, there is not much more elbow-room. Yet artificial restrictions on increase are un-desirable. They are the beginning of decay. Moreover there is not the slightest reason in our case to limit increase—provided the stock be sound—as long as there are vast undeveloped areas under our own flag simply clamouring for more and ever more inhabitants. We can and we ought to supply that need, and as a matter of fact there is a constant outflow of many of the most vigorous and enter-prising of our people to these new Britains beyond the seas. This stream of emigration is not an evil in itself. It is a good thing in itself. It would only become an evil if this precious human material, together with all that has gone before to the same regions, were to be lost to us and to the Empire. To prevent such a calamity, to keep the scattered communities of British stock, while severally inde-pendent within their own confines, one body politic among the sovereign nations of the world, maintaining their common history and traditions, and continuing to discharge their common duty to humanity—that is the noble, the difficult, but by no means im-possible task which Imperialism seeks to achieve.

Within that framework (he was writing in 1913) his mind was open to all ideas, because all ideas that proved to have any value at all could contribute, and were needed to contribute, to the great design.

In those last essays, *Questions of the Hour*, he tackled radically the great domestic problems, which for him were therefore Imperial problems, of the relations of capital with labour, of starvation in the midst of plenty, of taxation and economy, of state control and private enterprise. He was writing at the time of the blind rush back to what the Americans, perhaps wiser than they knew, called 'Normalcy'—wiser, because for a chimera they found a nightmare word. He was writing not as a professional agitator with an axe to grind, but as an elder statesman thinking aloud about the problems to be solved and the way they were being shirked: 'And in a case in which the wisest of us and those who speak with the highest authority in such matters—great men of business, learned economists—have gone astray along with the crowd, it is not presumptuous for any one to venture to think for himself, and to hesitate before he accepts the popular theories of the moment, even when they are backed by those to whose opinion under more normal conditions he might feel inclined to bow.'

Out of this unflinching humility came a series of ideas, many of which are now fully accepted, or beginning to be accepted, some of which anticipated the later findings of John Maynard Keynes. Not only ideas, but warnings which, had they been heeded, would have saved many tears. For the whole point about these ideas and these warnings is that they came not from an arm-chair theorist, not from a partisan fanatic, but from a practising statesman, a man of affairs, who knew the world and the people it was made of and how it worked—all from the first-hand experience of a lifetime at the heart of affairs. They were not heeded in the 'gay scramble' back to as-you-were.

Thus, of relations of capital with labour:

> The question whether Labour gets its fair share of what Labour produces is not the only question. Dig a little deeper and you come to the far more fundamental problem, whether our present national production is anything like as great as it ought to be. And, if it is not, where does the blame for the inadequacy of production rest? . . . For the real gravamen of the charge against our present industrial system is not that it involves an unfair distribution of the product, but that it mismanages, misdirects and therefore unduly limits production itself.

And again:

> . . . it is certain that many comforts and pleasures which formerly

were unknown or confined to a few, are now within the reach of millions. Yet, compared with the great and rapid growth of our capacity for production, the growth of prosperity, among the mass of the people, has been lamentably slow. . . . I find it perfectly impossible to believe that abject poverty . . . is the inevitable lot of any considerable number of people in this country under present conditions—that there must needs be men and women to be reckoned by the million who are underfed, underclothed, miserably housed, and lacking the barest necessities of health and comfort. It may be true, no doubt it is true, that we do not produce enough to supply their elementary needs. But why don't we? . . . Why, with so many wants unsatisfied, are so many hands idle that could help to satisfy them, and are only asking for the opportunity to do so? The existence side by side of all these unsatisfied wants and all that involuntary idleness must surely be due to some grave defect in social organisation.

He sought for the defect, and with a perfectly open mind. He found Labour partly to blame for the restriction of production, in terms now familiar to us all. But, while recording this fact, he found every excuse for the attitude of Labour and the Unions, and, moving over into a spirited defence of them, at once found himself involved in one of the strongest pleas for a controlled economy that has ever been made, beginning with a full-scale attack on the current system of distribution and the multiplicity of middlemen, and working through to the very conclusions recently reached by the post-war Conservative policy—but with this shining difference: that whereas the Conservatives have been forced into drawing up their celebrated Charters by the need of outbidding the Socialists and winning elections, Milner, caring neither for Socialists nor Conservatives as such, reached his conclusions twenty-five years ago by looking at the facts as he saw them and relating the needs of the day to his central idea: the survival of Britain and the Empire. In a word, his conclusions have a validity which the Conservative position, as expounded today, entirely lacks, because it is based not on conviction but upon expediency. Conversely, if the Conservatives of today can for one moment tear themselves away from the dubious game of outbidding the Socialists and go back a quarter of a century to

Questions of the Hour, and another decade to *The Nation and Empire*, they will find, ready-made, a foundation of solid reality which will support all that they are now trying to do, and more. It will, further, enable them to turn an assortment of half-assimilated and too frequently catch-penny slogans into a coherent policy which owes nothing at all to the philosophy of something-for-nothing and would give the country a sense of understanding and common purpose which it lacks. If the Conservatives cannot do this, then sooner or later the Socialists will do it for themselves: they are already moving in the required direction. But too slowly, and perhaps too late.

The misdirection of labour under the old system of free enterprise Milner took as axiomatic. He blamed nobody for the fearful waste involved in

> the huge army of salesmen, of advertisers, of brokers, of commission agents, whose activity is devoted to getting business for one firm at the expense of another. . . . They have often no choice but to get a living, as they do get it, by interception. But that the nation as a whole is the poorer through the diversion of so much energy from productive employment to the scramble for competitive distribution does not admit of doubt.

And again:

> Such results are inevitable as long as the investment of capital, determining as it does the nature and distribution of employment, is governed wholly by considerations of individual gain. Capital, in its constant search for profit, may often find or think it more advantageous to engage in financial operations which add nothing to the total wealth of the nation, than in promoting productive enterprise. . . . That is interception in the grand style. So are many, though not all, of the mergers, 'reconstructions', and so forth, with which we have become unpleasantly familiar. They have got to be paid for, in the long run, by the general public, which is therefore paying something for nothing.

He stresses and stresses again that 'from the point of view of the community, what matters is not only the total amount of production but a proper proportion between the different kinds of things produced. . . . The advance of the industrial army, if it is to be well sustained, must be an advance more or less in line. If one part of it gets too far ahead of the rest, there is dislocation and a general setback, in which all suffer.'

Then follows his defence of the workers' attitude in which, more than in any of his writings anywhere, he showed his deep understanding of the feelings and perplexities of common humanity, an understanding which throughout his life he was unable to communicate except to those closest to him:

> When one of these setbacks, whatever is the cause, occurs, the wage-earners are the chief, though not the only, sufferers. But what lends poignancy to their sufferings, what indeed is the main cause of their unrest, is their sense of complete helplessness in the matter. They are the victims of transactions over which they could exercise no possible control. They have nothing whatever to say to the direction of capital, upon which their employment depends, yet they may at any moment be reduced to penury by its misdirection. No doubt the misdirection of capital brings loss to the capitalist himself as well as to the labourer, but then he has nobody but himself to blame. . . . The workman's grievance is that he, too, has to pay the piper, though he has never had the fun of calling the tune. . . . He may be too ignorant to understand the causes of the 'bad times' of which he is the victim. But he is apt to suspect, and, as we have seen, with some reason, that they are not due to inexorable Fate, but in great part at least to human blundering, not to say human dishonesty. And those blunders, whoever may have been responsible for them, were certainly not his. They were made by those who had the power, as he has not, of steering the ship of industry and who ought not, as he thinks, to have steered it on to the rocks.

And:

> . . . amid all the half-baked schemes and conflicting counsels which characterise the attack upon 'Capitalism', one dominant idea emerges and persists, and will have to be reckoned with. This is the conviction that, as long as capital is the master and not the servant of productive industry, the majority of mankind derives no adequate benefit from its accumulation.

And:

> Just as soldiers will never fight their best if they have lost faith in the skill of their general, so men will not work their best if they

doubt the competence of those by whom their work is directed. And the more educated and intelligent the workman is, the more critical he is. For good or evil, it must be recognised that we have to deal with a more critical body of workers. And this is true not only of individual businesses, but of industry as a whole. Labour is more and more inclined to question the competence of the bigwigs of industry and finance. There is a loss of confidence in the management.

It is impossible in these pages to follow Milner's argument in all its detail, or to convey the severely restrained impatience and indignation which at times brings a curious glow to the grey surface of his prose. He demanded experiment. He demanded an absolute rejection of the belief that we were producing as much as we could. The fundamental question as he saw it was 'how to combine the economic advantages of large-scale production with that keenness and feeling of personal responsibility in the individual worker, that pride and pleasure in his work, which belonged of old days to the independent craftsman'. And he thought that the solution probably lay in 'the association of producers in groups either having capital of their own or sufficient credit to borrow it'.

'The form of industrial organisation which prevails today', he said categorically, 'is not so perfect that mankind is likely to reject any practical alternative which could show better results. There is nothing sacred or final about the Joint Stock Company system. It has its place, no doubt, and performs a useful function in our present state of economic development. But no extraordinary power of imagination is required to picture a future in which we could get on without it.'

It is in this context that he recalled his own phrase about Labour hiring Capital instead of Capital hiring Labour.

As a matter of fact the idea is neither novel nor revolutionary. It is as old as the hills. What is new, or at least modern, a product of the Industrial Revolution, is the divorce of those actually engaged in productive work from the ownership and control of the materials and instruments of production. At a certain stage of industrial development that divorce became inevitable, but it does not follow that we should necessarily regard it as permanent. It is surely conceivable, as it is in every respect to be desired, that the people actually engaged in any industry should themselves be its capitalists, or, in so far as they should need the assistance of external capital, should pay for the use of it, without becoming subject to the control of its possessors.

Chapter Nineteen

THE CONSTRUCTIVE IDEA

WE HAVE BEEN trying rather to fix a quality of mind and to establish its central idea, than to give a summary of that mind's conclusions, which can be found in other places. Thus it would be out of place to examine the suggestions put forward by Milner for overcoming the social and industrial problems posed in the last chapter. He argued closely the case for Joint Industrial Councils, for example. He saw the need for some sort of an Industrial Parliament. He touched on other solutions very much in the air just now. But it is, to repeat, the quality of the mind which in this study we have sought to explore. That this quality was, to say the least, unusual should by now be clear. Some of the passages on industry and society quoted in the last chapter are passages which any Socialist would be proud to have written. But they were not written by a Socialist. They were written by 'the man who made the Boer War'. Some of the passages on Imperialism and the white man's burden might have been written by a Tory diehard. But they were not written by a Tory diehard. They were written by the student of Karl Marx.

There is no schizophrenia here—and this is the crux. There is no split personality, no change of heart from decade to decade. Some who knew Milner in his later years, and found it hard to reconcile the social reformer with the legendary strong and rigid autocrat, used to say that he had 'mellowed'. But he had not mellowed at all—not in the sense it was intended to convey. His mind was all of a piece, and it was all of a piece all his life. If some of his ideas seemed incompatible to many, this was no more than a reflection of the way in which most minds are limited by conventional moulds. He never took ideas on trust: an idea, a conception, to him was not an idea until it could work its own

169

passage. That meant that as an Imperialist he instinctively rejected all the clutter of conceptions which are popularly supposed to go with Imperialism. It meant that as a social reformer he rejected all the common conventions which have arisen simply out of un-thinking reaction to the ruling ideas. He possessed in a very high degree the faculty of disassociation. This is a faculty usually found in the artist, whose mind is free and unprejudiced and open to the direct impact of experience. But with this (and the combina-tion is one of the rarest in the world) he possessed the faculty of re-association. This is a faculty usually found in men of action, who have no time to analyse but excel in synthesis.

Everything he touched received first the impact of his scepti-cism and then the impulse of his hope. It was not enough for him to pull established ideas to pieces because they did not work. He had to put them together again so that this time they did work. Thus, in a great campaign which went on for years to get what would now be called a fair deal for British agriculture, he was not content to combat the familiar arguments for its neglect: he had to go to the roots of the state of mind behind those arguments: '... And if it be said that it "would not pay" to cultivate the land better, my answer is that that may be true for the individual farmer, but it cannot be true for the community. That it is good business for a nation, of which only a minority is productively employed, to buy enormous quantities of goods which it has the means of producing for itself, is a contention repugnant to common sense. And if it is true that under present conditions it "does not pay" to make proper use of the greatest of our national resources, there is urgent need to consider how we have got ourselves into that lamentable position!'

And when he is tackling the problem of free trade versus protection (even though his immediate aim, as in the words that follow, is to urge the Labour Party not to follow the Liberals) we find precisely the same radical approach:

> ... there are at least two reasons why, as it seems to me, it is dangerous for the Labour Party to accept 'buying in the cheapest market' as the golden rule of conduct, or to admit that cheapness, whatever its cause or its consequences, is always a blessing.

For, in the first place, such a doctrine completely negatives the idea that there is such a thing as a just wage, or a just price for anything. But, this idea once abandoned, it is hard to see what can prevent unrestricted competition from trampling first one and then another set of workers into the dust. It is agriculture today, but it may be any other of our staple industries tomorrow. The conception of price as an instrument for effecting a fair exchange of the products of one industry for those of another—taking into account what is required for the due reward of labour in each—entirely disappears.

Somewhere, governing the free approach to all the problems of his time and fusing together effortlessly ideas which are not normally fused together, there is a common denominator or a guiding principle. It is not hard to find. Indeed, we run into it at every turn. It is love of country—and belief in country. It is far from being, as we have seen, an uncritical love. The convinced Imperialist could write: 'But if the question is asked, how much, beyond giving it just laws and honest administration, Great Britain has done for her vast dependent Empire, a true answer cannot be altogether flattering to our national pride. The economic backwardness of the Empire is indeed a discredit alike to our generosity and our intelligence. . . . Who can contemplate without some feeling of shame the economic decay of the British West Indies, the oldest oversea possessions of the British Crown?'

And the man who called the spirit of class enmity 'the greatest bar to Social Progress' could go on to write: 'That there are great defects in our social system, which inevitably engender class enmity, is undeniable. But it is not to subversive doctrines imported from abroad, but to moral forces of native growth, that we should look for the building up of a better Social Order. And among the strongest of these forces is patriotism—pride in our country, which must make us loathe the spectacle of the degrading conditions in which so many of its people are still condemned to live. What a source of national weakness! What a stain on the national honour!'

The idea of patriotism, except in war, has been barred in the most articulate circles for something like the lifetime of the present writer. Even in war it was not encouraged: we were fighting for something bigger and nobler than country—though nobody knew quite what. For humanity? And what was humanity? The prisoners in the Russian labour camps? Or the people who put them where they are? . . . The idea behind the idea, of course, was admirable, as far as it went—which was not very far. The idea was that self-assertion and the assumption of authority were retrogressive and unedifying. Perhaps they are. But the Politburo does not think so. And nor, if it comes to that, do many Americans—who think, for example, that the British Empire is a very bad thing and do all they can to bring it to an end. President Roosevelt was one of these.

Now, at something like the eleventh hour, we begin to see that if relative good refuses to assert itself, relative evil all too gladly will. It is at this stage that we find ourselves crying for an idea. But it is no good as a nation believing in ideas unless we first believe in ourselves. Looking round the world today, that should not prove too hard. If we can do it with sufficient single-mindedness, as Milner did, then the very effort to sustain that belief will, as it did with Milner, generate all the ideas we can possibly require.

INDEX

Adams, Goold, 10

Agriculture: plans to develop in South Africa, 99; problems of, 170

America, United States of: their way of life, 139

Amery, L. S., 82, 134, 141

Appeasement, policy of, 35, 62, 102

Asquith, Herbert (later Earl of Oxford and Asquith), 16, 30, 107; on Milner, 27, 50

Baldwin, Stanley (later Earl Baldwin), 128–9, 130, 131, 132, 147–8

Balfour, Arthur (later Earl of Balfour), 111, 112, 128, 129

Balliol College, Oxford, 15–16

Baynes, Hamilton, Bishop, 108

Behaviour, necessity for common code of, 140–1

Bermondsey, 21

Bloemfontein Conference, 85, 88, 137

Boers, the, 29, 32; need for force in dealing with, 4, 10; revolt at Majuba Hill, 46, 50; secret arming of, 47, 50–1, 91; ultimatum of October 1899, 51; love of power, 78; hatred and suspicion of Britain, 78; thwarting of reconciliation policy after War, 104; 1907 majority in Transvaal, 113

Boer War, 38, 43, 44 ff.; causes, 48, 49; pro-Boer feeling, 44

Bonn, 12

Botha, Louis, 113

British, the: influence of, 29; powers of leadership of, 33; attitude to native question, 47; benefits under their rule, 72; coming gradually to idea of war with Kruger, 88; qualities of, 121–5; mental inertia of, 127, 133

British Empire, the: significance of, 100–1; problem of maintaining unity in, 124–5

British Guiana Ordinance for importation of Indian coolies, 107

Buller, Sir Redvers, General, 59, 66, 93

Burns, John, 22

Butler, Sir William, Lt.-General, 65, 66–7, 93

Byles, William, 112

Cape Colony, 27; British right to, 45–6; importance to Britain of, 49; treachery of their government, 62, 66, 68; disloyal Dutch in, 70, 71; Milner's encouragement to loyalists, 74; and the Bloemfontein Conference, 85

Cape Town, 10, 51, 52

Capital, relations of with Labour, 162, 163–4, 166–8

Cecil, Lady Edward (later Lady Milner), 9, 96, 97, 137

Chamberlain, Joseph, 10, 59, 61, 65, 67, 77, 79–80, 82, 88, 93, 112, 133, 135; indispensable to Milner's policy, 128; Milner's appreciation of, 90